THE
KINGDOM
OF
GOD
IN YOU

RELEASING
THE KINGDOM

—

REPLENISHING
THE EARTH

REVISED & UPDATED

THE
KINGDOM
OF
GOD
IN YOU

RELEASING
THE KINGDOM

REPLENISHING
THE EARTH

DR. BILL WINSTON

Unless otherwise identified, Scripture quotations are taken from the King James Version of the Bible. Scripture quotations marked New King James Version. Copyright © 1982 by Thomas Nelson, Inc. Used by permission. All rights reserved. Scripture quotations marked AMP are taken from the Amplified® Bible, Classic Edition, Copyright © 1954, 1958, 1962, 1964, 1965, 1987 by The Lockman Foundation. All rights reserved. Used by permission. Scripture quotations marked NLT are taken from the Holy Bible, New Living Translation, copyright 1996, 2004, 2015. Used by permission of Tyndale House Publishers, Wheaton, Illinois 60189. All rights reserved.

Previously published under ISBN 13: 978-1-57794-796-7

Published by Harrison House Publishers, Shippensburg, PA 17257

ISBN 13 TP: 978-1-6803-1703-9

ISBN 13 eBook: 978-1-6803-1704-6

ISBN 13 HC: 978-1-6803-1706-0

ISBN 13 LP: 978-1-6803-1705-3

For Worldwide Distribution, Printed in the U.S.A.

3 4 5 6 7 8 / 25 24 23 22

CONTENTS

FOREWORD

But seek ye first the kingdom of God, and his righteousness; and all these things shall be added unto you.

—MATTHEW 6:33

The Lord Jesus made it clear what our priority in life should be when He said, "Seek ye first the kingdom of God and his righteousness." Many of us have known this verse of Scripture for a long time but haven't realized that it contains the power to change the world. This is why Jesus spoke so frequently about the kingdom of God. The Bible tells us, in fact, that before His ascension Jesus spent forty days preaching the gospel of the kingdom. (See Acts 1:3.) There must have been something to that message if it consumed His final forty days of ministry on earth.

In order to make the kingdom of God our first priority as Jesus taught us, we need to cut through the mystery surrounding it and uncover the truth God wants to reveal to us through His Word. We can only go as high as the revelation we've received, so we must look into the Scriptures to enter the kingdom life that God has provided for us. From Genesis to Revelation God has revealed the secrets of His kingdom.

Through the Scriptures the whole kingdom is in sight. Jesus revealed to His disciples how to live in the kingdom of God even while they walked the earth. When we receive this revelation and begin to act on it, we will see the kingdom at work in the earth even in our own lives.

Each of us is a vital part of the kingdom of God. As we study the Scriptures, the Holy Spirit will begin to lay a foundation in our hearts that the devil cannot shake. We will learn how to operate in the kingdom of God, which will provide everything we need in life to fulfill our God-given calling—everything from wisdom and understanding to peace, joy, health, abundant provision, and so much more.

This book is not for the complacent who desire the status quo. This is a soul-changing message that will turn the timid into the bold! It will result in miracles that will build God's kingdom right here and right now. Read on, because God wants to reveal *The Kingdom of God in Us.*

INTRODUCTION

In the first edition of this ground-breaking book, *The Kingdom of God in You*, I shared truths from the Word of God that (I believe) had been widely overlooked by many in the church. At the time, only a handful of preachers were teaching on the kingdom, even though the gospel of the kingdom was the main message that Jesus preached while here on the earth.

The importance of the kingdom of God cannot be underestimated. The body of Christ must make advancing the kingdom its first priority, especially in this present season when so many are filled with fear and hopelessness. Jesus Christ and the kingdom He brought to the earth are still the answer to every problem facing humanity. The kingdom of God is the *supernatural* government of heaven that carries the power and authority to override the curse that entered the earth through Adam's disobedience. When the kingdom comes, Satan's kingdom of darkness, set up through "fallen man," is overturned and rapidly displaced.

The kingdom of God must be taught for people to believe and have faith in its power. Nothing in the kingdom or the promises found in the Bible are automatic. They require faith in the heart of the believer. Romans 10:14 says, "How then shall they call on him in whom they have not believed? and how shall they believe in him of whom they have not heard? and how shall they hear without a preacher?"

This is why Jesus preached the good news of the kingdom of God from the beginning of His ministry until the time He was taken up to heaven, "Now after that John was put in prison, Jesus came into Galilee, preaching the gospel of the kingdom of God, and saying, The time is fulfilled, and the kingdom of God is at hand: repent ye, and believe the gospel" (Mark 1:14–15).

Later, in the Book of Acts, the scripture says, "During the forty days after he (Jesus) suffered and died, he appeared to the apostles from time to time... And he talked to them about the kingdom of God" (Acts 1:1:3 NLT). Why did Jesus talk to them about the kingdom? Because the apostles and disciples who would later follow Him were to continue preaching this message after Jesus was taken back up into Heaven. The apostle Paul taught about the kingdom of God, "And he went into the synagogue, and spake boldly for the space of three months, disputing and persuading the things concerning the kingdom of God" (Acts 19:8).

The kingdom of God was the disciples' main message, and God confirmed it by miracles, signs and wonders. Through this message, the early church "turned the world upside down" in their day, and it's the same message for you and me, and all the church to be the world changers of our day, no matter our denomination or ministry affiliation. We are still living in the church age and we must finish Jesus' work by demonstrating the gospel of the kingdom of God. We must fulfill our God-given, kingdom assignments wherever our King sends us.

In this expanded edition of *The Kingdom of God in You: Releasing the Kingdom, Replenishing the Earth,* I share additional revelation that God has given me since the first book was published. This book you are about to read builds upon the revelation in Luke 17:20-21, "And when he was demanded of the Pharisees, when the kingdom of God should come, he answered them and said, The kingdom of God cometh not with observation: neither shall they say, Lo here! or, lo there! for, behold, the kingdom of God is within you."

There is nothing more powerful than the kingdom of God. Psalm 103:19 says, "The Lord has prepared his throne in the heavens; and his kingdom ruleth over all." Nothing can stop kingdom progress and expansion when the Word of the kingdom (God's Word) is released by faith in the mouth of a believer. It will uproot anything, anywhere, at any time that was not in God's original plan to bring heaven to earth. This includes sickness and disease, lack and poverty, strife and division, and everything brought by the curse after Adam committed high treason by disobeying God in the Garden of Eden.

In *The Kingdom of God in You: Releasing the Kingdom, Replenishing the Earth,* you will learn:

- Through the kingdom, God has provided everything we will ever need here on

5

earth—understanding, wisdom, peace, joy, health, prosperity, provision, and protection. Therefore, we don't need to fret or worry about anything.

- The job of the Holy Spirit, who lives inside of every born-again believer, is to help us fulfill our purpose here on the earth and to access every natural and supernatural thing that we need to reach our destiny. The Holy Spirit is our tutor. As our tutor, the Holy Spirit perfects our Christian walk and character, so that our presence and activity in the world are a true expression and representation of Christ's nature and character.

- The Bible is the constitution of the kingdom of God. It tells us our rights and privileges as kingdom citizens, and what is available to us in earth and in heaven.

- Real prosperity is the ability to use God's ability to meet any need – spiritually, physically, emotionally, socially or financially—independent of our circumstances.

- Everything in the kingdom operates by faith. "As it is written, The just shall live by faith" (Rom. 1:17). We must believe that the kingdom is in us and that we are in the kingdom through our faith in Jesus Christ.

- And, the law of sowing and reaping is the platform by which all of the other kingdom principles work.

As you read this newly expanded edition, my desire is that God will open your eyes and give you a greater understanding of the kingdom of God and your role in it. Like the Apostle Paul, I pray "that the God of our Lord Jesus Christ, the Father of glory, may give unto you the spirit of wisdom and revelation in the knowledge of him" and of His kingdom (Eph. 1:17). I encourage you to pray this prayer for yourself. When you do, get ready to experience signs, wonders and miracles not yet experienced by you and those around you. Why? Because the kingdom of God is in you.

CHAPTER 1

A CITIZEN OF
THE KINGDOM

Y ou could have been born in the 1800s or sometime in the
future, but you were born into the earth in this generation
for such a time as this. Why? Because God has a special kingdom assignment for you to fulfill.

A STRATEGIC POSITIONING AND TIME

Know this, never before has it been so important for us to be
mature believers, appointed and anointed to take our place in
the earth and in the church. I have been preaching the gospel of
the kingdom throughout the world for decades to teach believers how to live independent of this world's system and have
dominion over it. We are called to demonstrate the goodness of
God and the power of His kingdom. We are not to be beggars
or orphans, but rather, according to Deuteronomy, chapter 28,

we are to be the head and the lenders, having enough financial strength to meet the budgets of nations.

As we've been learning, the kingdom of God is in you. This kingdom or government is the source of every provision that you will need in the earth until Jesus comes. Are you experiencing the goodness and power of His kingdom in your own life and demonstrating it to others? Or have you been you struggling with sickness, family problems, or living paycheck to paycheck? If this latter situation describes your life, know that God has much better plans for you, and it starts with knowing who you are and what is on the inside of you.

GOD HAS CALLED YOU TO LIVE ABOVE THE WORLD

Here is what the Apostle Paul wrote to the church in Corinth who thought they were so spiritual because they spoke in tongues and operated in the gifts of the Holy Spirit (See 1 Corinthians, chapter 12.):

> *And I, brethren, could not speak unto you as unto spiritual, but as unto carnal, even as unto babes in Christ.*
>
> 1 CORINTHIANS 3:1

As unto what? Babes. In other words, even though you got saved, you never grew. Paul goes on to say, "I have fed you with milk, and not with meat: for hitherto ye were not able to bear it, neither yet now are ye able. For ye are yet carnal: for whereas there is among you envying, and strife, and divisions, are ye not carnal, and walk as men?" (vv. 2- 3).

"For ye are yet carnal: for whereas there is among you envying," (I'll add some words to this list: jealousy, backbiting, gossiping) "and strife and divisions" (black, white, you don't like me, I don't like you, racism). Divisions could mean thinking more of a particular denomination or group than you do of the body of Christ.

YOU ARE NOT JUST HUMAN

"Are ye not carnal...and walk as men?" *The Amplified Bible* says, "behaving yourselves after a human standard and like mere (unchanged) men." Some people call themselves "Christians" yet still walk, talk and behave like unbelievers.

You are not just human. The unsaved in the world are, but you're not if you've been born again. Why? God is in you. Say this aloud, "God is in me now."

You've got to say those words, get them down in your heart, and believe it! Once you get this revelation, no force of darkness will be able to stop you or steal from you.

SATAN DOESN'T WANT YOU TO UNDERSTAND THE KINGDOM

In Matthew, chapter 13, Jesus tells the story of the sower.

Behold, a sower went forth to sow; and when he sowed, some seeds fell by the way side, and the fowls came and devoured them up: some fell upon stony places, where they had not much earth: and forthwith they sprung up, because they had no deepness of earth: and when the sun was up, they were scorched; and because they had no

11

root, they withered away. And some fell among thorns; and the thorns sprung up, and choked them: but other fell into good ground, and brought forth fruit, some an hundredfold, some sixtyfold, some thirtyfold.

VERSES 3–8

What is the sower sowing? Seed. What seed? Luke 8:11 says, "The seed is the word of God," which He could give you in the form of a new idea.

Now look at verse 12 in Matthew, chapter 13, "For whosoever hath, to him shall be given, and he shall have more abundance: but whosoever hath not, from him shall be taken away even that he hath."

What "more abundance" is Jesus talking about? Understanding of the kingdom. The verse goes on to say, "But whosoever hath not, from him shall be taken away even that he hath." Hath not what? Understanding the kingdom of God.

Jesus ends the story by saying, "Hear ye therefore the parable of the sower. When any one heareth the word of the kingdom..." (Matt. 13:18–19). Notice, Jesus calls the seed—the Word of the kingdom.

For example, when our church was located at Luke and Pulaski Streets in Chicago in the early days of the ministry, a woman came asking for how to deal with drug dealers who had taken over her block. We immediately got into a circle to pray for a Word of the kingdom (the Bible says come boldly to the throne of grace). God gave me a word that she was to take a bottle of anointing oil and pour it down the street of her city block. She took the oil and acted on the Word of the king-dom, which resulted in the drug dealers coming out for one hour the next day (before then they were coming out for 12 hours every day), and left never coming back. She did not call the local police department, nor did she form a neighborhood block club. She only received the Word of the kingdom, which when acted on released the power of God's government to perform. Now you can see how the operation of the kingdom guarantees unfailing results.

YOU ARE A CITIZEN IN THE KINGDOM OF GOD

We, who have been born again, are kingdom citizens. Philippians 3:20 NLT says, "We are citizens of heaven, where the Lord Jesus Christ lives. And we are eagerly waiting for him to return as our Savior." Our citizenship is in heaven.

We are first kingdom citizens before we are members of a local church or a certain denomination. How did I get my citizenship? I had to be born into it. In natural citizenship, people can come from Russia, or Mexico, or Nigeria, and get a U.S. citizenship by filling out forms and passing certain tests. But in the kingdom of God, you can't do that; you've got to be supernaturally born into the kingdom. So, I'm a citizen first because that is how I was born. After we become a citizen in the kingdom of God, then God directs us to a local church where we become a member.

YOU ARE AN AMBASSADOR FOR CHRIST

You and I are also ambassadors of the King and His kingdom. "Now then we are ambassadors for Christ, as though God did beseech you by us: we pray you in Christ's stead, be ye reconciled to God" (2 Cor. 5:20).

So, as a child of God and a citizen of the kingdom, you are sent as an ambassador to take care of diplomatic business in the earth on behalf of your King. You are here to represent Jesus, and you are limited only to speak what your government has declared and what your constitution has allowed.

And, just in case you don't know what He said, He's given you the Word of the kingdom in the Bible. His Word is also your "Bill of Rights," which tells what your benefits are and what God promises to do for you.

It's Time to Step Out of the Box

As a kingdom citizen, you have to get your direction from God and obey what He tells you to do and where He tells you to go.

The world's system, "ruled by the god of this world," is designed to intimidate you. It does not want you to think freely, creatively, or have one "Bible thought." In Satan's system, you are not supposed to think outside of his box. But if anyone is supposed to think outside that box, it's God's people – the church! Without God's thoughts and imagination, the church will not be able to advance the kingdom of God and "possess the land" that God has given us.

Let me give a personal example. Several years ago, God gave me a vision to start a bank so that Christians could have a place where their money could help spread the gospel, support Christian businesses and entrepreneurship, and reinvest in communities. Sadly, it wasn't the unbelievers who came against this vision, but leaders in some local churches. I'm not coming down on anyone because here's my point: When Christians, even leaders, don't understand the kingdom of God, and who they are as kingdom citizens, even they can come against you and the mission that God has assigned for you to accomplish. Biblically, you can see that in the life of the Apostle Paul and even Jesus. (See Acts 23:12; John, chapter 9; 2 Timothy 3:12.)

WHEN YOU UNDERSTAND YOUR KINGDOM CITIZENSHIP, YOU CAN DO WHAT GOD HAS GIVEN YOU TO DO

Again, we're ambassadors of Christ and citizens of the kingdom of God first. We're not to promote our denomination but the gospel of the kingdom. God does plant believers in local churches for spiritual covering, discipleship, and fellowship; however, it's when we get revelation and understanding of our citizenship in the kingdom of God that we can accomplish what God has assigned us to do for His glory.

GENESIS MANDATE

God revealed His purpose for us, His children, in Genesis 1:26.

> *And God said, Let us make man in our image, after our likeness: and let them have dominion over the fish of the sea, and over the fowl of the air, and over the cattle, and over all the earth, and over every creeping thing that creepeth upon the earth.*
>
> GENESIS 1:26

He made Adam and Eve in His image and likeness and gave them dominion over everything He had created. From the beginning, God's plan was always to bring heaven to earth and

15

recreate the Garden of Eden throughout the planet. His plan has never changed.

Like heaven, God provided in the garden of Eden everything that Adam and Eve would ever desire, including peace, love, and perfect fellowship with the Father. The kingdom of God, though invisible, operates the same way today.

God told us how to fulfill our purpose on the earth in Genesis 1:28.

> *And God blessed them, and God said unto them, Be fruitful, and multiply, and replenish the earth, and subdue it: and have dominion over the fish of the sea, and over the fowl of the air, and over every living thing that moveth upon the earth.*

In this verse, to bless means "to empower for success or empower to prosper." When God blessed Adam and Eve, He conferred on them the power He used to create the universe, which is called "The Blessing." After God blessed them, He then gave them four principles of creation to dominate and rule the planet—be fruitful, multiply, replenish the earth, and subdue it. When you meditate on Genesis 1:28 until it becomes a revelation, it will transform your thinking and empower you, as a kingdom citizen, to fulfill your God-given assignment in the earth.

"BE FRUITFUL"

"Be fruitful" were the first words that Adam heard God speak in the Garden of Eden. These words weren't a suggestion, but a command, and they carried the power to bring themselves to pass. (See Genesis 1:3,11.)

To be fruitful means "to produce, to create, to make public, or to bring forth." What was God commanding Adam to bring forth? Everything He had planned for the earth and mankind before the world was created. When God told Adam to "be fruitful," He expected Adam to create in the earth what He had already created in heaven and stored in heaven's warehouse. God expects this same fruitfulness or creativity from us today.

Being fruitful has to do with God producing through each one of us a product or service or idea that will benefit mankind and establish His kingdom here on earth. And because God mandated us to be fruitful, He is obligated to give us ideas (seed).

Each of us are made in the image of our Creator, having the same spiritual DNA to bring forth creatively something new. Wherever you work, in government, education, technology or entertainment, expect the seeds or ideas that would answer your call or mandate to be fruitful as a co-laborer with God.

Fruitfulness will enable you to bring forth heaven's solutions—products, services, ideas, technologies, and innovations conceived and created from another realm (the eternal) that have never been seen before. That is, you will think thoughts that were in the mind of your Creator before the foundation of the world...thoughts and ideas that will lift humanity and glorify God.

Psalm 72:18 says, "Blessed be the Lord God, the God of Israel, who only doeth wondrous things." The word *wondrous* is described in some Bible commentaries as "great wonders that no one can match; works that leave all others behind." Wondrous works are what happen when we follow God's commands as kingdom citizens to bring forth heaven's ideas and plans into the earth.

EVERYTHING CHANGES WHEN
THE KINGDOM COMES

Again, God's kingdom is a government, and if you're born again, you have kingdom authority. God has called you to rule where He's placed you, which includes the command to "be fruitful, multiply, replenish the earth, and subdue it."

God's mandate for us to subdue the earth includes not only bringing salvation and restoration to individuals, but to cities and nations. When you come on the scene as a citizen of the kingdom, everything changes. Why? Because the kingdom of God is in you. All of it!

All of the kingdom can be in me, and all of it can be in you at the same time. What is this kingdom going to do? It's going to provide and bring to you everything you have ever needed independent of the circumstances around you. And, as I said at the opening of this chapter, it will also empower you to create such wealth that you will be able to meet the budgets of nations!

CHAPTER 2

OUT OF THE DARKNESS, INTO THE LIGHT

While sojourning this earth, Jesus taught extensively about the kingdom of God. His disciple Luke wrote,

The former treatise have I made, O Theophilus, of all that Jesus began both to do and teach, until the day in which he was taken up, after that he through the Holy Ghost had given commandments unto the apostles whom he had chosen: To whom also he shewed himself alive after his passion by many infallible proofs, being seen of them forty days, and speaking of the things pertaining to the kingdom of God.

ACTS 1:1-3

Again, forty days after His resurrection, Jesus was still teaching about the kingdom of God. There must have been some significance to that message if He took that kind of time to teach about it. And He taught us to seek first the kingdom of God. That means our highest priority is supposed to be seeking the kingdom.

How do we seek the kingdom? Well, we don't do it by looking around and saying, "kingdom, where are you?"

TWO KINGDOMS

Colossians 1:13 says, "[God] hath delivered us from the power of darkness, and hath translated us into the kingdom of his dear Son." When Jesus becomes our Lord and Savior, we are translated out of the kingdom of darkness and into the kingdom of God.

In Matthew 12:25 Jesus says, "Every kingdom divided against itself is brought to desolation; and every city or house divided against itself shall not stand." This means the kingdom of God has an enemy that can divide us. Jesus and Satan both have kingdoms, and they are opposed to one another.

Satan is the head of the kingdom of darkness. For the most part, he has been the agent behind the systems of this world. Jesus, who is the head of the kingdom of light, reveals Satan's deception in John 8:30-33:

As [Jesus] spake these words, many believed on him. Then said Jesus to those Jews which believed on him, If ye continue in my word, then are ye my disciples indeed; and ye shall know the truth, and the truth shall make you free. They answered him, We be Abraham's seed, and were never in bondage to any man: how sayest thou, Ye shall be made free?

Satan deceives religious people into believing they are free, or in right standing with God, when they are actually in captivity. These Jews believed they were free simply because they were born Jews and were the seed of Abraham. The truth being that they were in bondage to the kingdom of darkness, which manifested in their being under occupation by the Roman governments, but they didn't even realize it. Today, many people—including those claiming the Christian faith and other religions—are bound in the kingdom of darkness, but they don't know it because the enemy has deceived them.

Jesus further reveals the devil's hidden schemes in verse 44, saying,

> *Ye are of your father the devil, and the lusts of your father ye will do. He was a murderer from the beginning, and abode not in the truth, because there is no truth in him. When he speaketh a lie, he speaketh of his own: for he is a liar, and the father of it.*

Jesus is saying that the enemy puts pressure on people to cooperate with his evil system, and they are often unaware of it because it is so pervasive. He lies to them, and they believe his lies and perpetuate his lies through deception. Then they become liars. Once Jesus has translated us into His kingdom at the new birth (John 3:3), God wants us to know what the devil is doing and separate ourselves from his kingdom and its way of doing things. He wants to expose and break the strongholds that have held people in bondage to the world's system. He wants to train us to reign in this earth and take dominion, and become witnesses of the kingdom of God.

A CALL TO SEPARATION

In Matthew 3, John the Baptist begins to preach about the two kingdoms.

> *In those days came John the Baptist preaching in the wilderness of Judea and saying, Repent ye: for the kingdom of heaven is at hand.*
>
> MATTHEW 3:1-2

John called people to repent—to turn away from sin and their old way of doing things—and to seek God and His way of doing things. He was saying, essentially, "Change your way of thinking and turn to God. Come out of the kingdom of darkness and enter the kingdom of God."

The people in Israel at this time were under the Law of Moses. They kept the laws and sacrificed their livestock for their atonement. They depended on the high priest to mediate between themselves and God. Now John the Baptist comes along and says, "A new day is coming!" Jeremiah also prophesied this new day:

> *Behold, the days come, saith the Lord, that I will make a new covenant with the house of Israel, and with the house of Judah: not according to the covenant that I made with their fathers in the day that I took them by the hand to bring them out of the land of Egypt; which my covenant they brake, although I was an husband unto them, saith the Lord: but this shall be the covenant that I will make with the house of Israel; after those days, saith the Lord, I will put my law in their*

inward parts, and write it in their hearts; and will be their God, and they shall be my people.

And they shall teach no more every man his neighbour, and every man his brother, saying, Know the Lord: for they shall all know me, from the least of them unto the greatest of them, saith the Lord: for I will forgive their iniquity, and I will remember their sin no more.

JEREMIAH 31:31-34

Jeremiah was prophesying about the Messiah's entrance into the earth. He was saying, "Jesus is coming." (*Jesus* means "Jehovah is salvation.") This is what John the Baptist was announcing to the Jews. Their Messiah was here! John had what I call a "transition ministry": He was leading God's people out of the system of the Old Covenant Law and into the system of grace. He was a prophet, preparing the Jews to receive the Messiah, the Anointed One. He was tearing up hard ground in their hearts and softening them to receive the engrafted Word of God, Jesus, who would change their hearts and lives forever.

The evidence that they had received John's ministry and message was their being baptized. This showed that they were willing to turn from trying to do things on their own and turn to dependence on God. They were turning from the system of this world to the system of the kingdom of God.

This is what God wants us to do today. Even if we have accepted Jesus as our Lord and Savior, we still have to turn from the system of this world in order to live in the reality of God's kingdom.

TRANSLATED INTO GOD'S KINGDOM

The Father sent Jesus into the earth carrying government, the kingdom of God on His shoulders (Isa. 9:6). In John 18:36, Jesus said, "My kingdom is not of this world." Jesus is the King of the kingdom of God. When we were saved, we were translated out of the kingdom of darkness into His kingdom.

The only way into the kingdom of God and to experience the kingdom life is to be born into it. When the Bible says we must be born again, in the original Greek it says we must be born from above.[1] We are actually born from heaven—another government, another country—the kingdom of God.

Jesus prayed, "As my Father hath sent me, even so send I you" (John 20:21). Once we are in His kingdom, Jesus sends us out into the world to represent Him. Paul said in 2 Corinthians 5:20, "Now are you ambassadors for Christ."

Jesus is the King, and we are His ambassadors. An ambassador is sent to a foreign nation to represent the king. We are Christ's ambassadors, sent to represent Him and take care of diplomatic business on His behalf. When we come into the land, we don't say, "Well, I think...." No, we say, "Jesus said. "

We call His name. Colossians 3:17 says, "Whatsoever ye do in word or deed, do all in the name of the Lord Jesus."

We are representatives of Jesus in this world. When Jesus was on earth and physically ministering, He preached the gospel of the kingdom and met everyone's needs. Then He said,

> *It is expedient for you that I go away: for if I go not away, the Comforter will not come unto you; but if I depart, I will send him unto you.*
>
> JOHN 16:7

Jesus was going away and sending the Holy Spirit to dwell inside every kingdom citizen. While He walked the earth, the Holy Spirit was in Him. However, Jesus' physical body was limited to one location, so the effectiveness of the Holy Spirit was limited.

Today, through the body of Christ, the Holy Spirit can saturate the whole earth. When the Holy Spirit came into the earth after Jesus' ascension, He set up residence inside of every believer. Once we are born again, the Comforter lives inside us. We come into the kingdom of God, and at the same time the kingdom of God comes inside of us.

As believers, we have the whole kingdom of God inside of us. God's plan is for the kingdom of God to spread throughout the entire earth through the body of Christ. This explains why Jesus said,

> *He that believeth on me, the works that I do shall he do also...that he may abide with you for ever.*
>
> JOHN 14:12,16

Jesus was saying that we could do the works He did and greater works, or more works, by the Holy Spirit coming to live inside many believers. The Holy Spirit made the whole kingdom available to all who would believe on Jesus. As believers, we now have the kingdom in us, and through us the Holy Spirit will cause the kingdom to manifest in earth as it is in heaven.

EVERYTHING IS INSIDE

In the kingdom God has provided everything we need here on earth—understanding, wisdom, peace, joy, health, prosperity, provision, and protection. The Holy Spirit is within us to help us access every natural and supernatural thing we need.

This is why Jesus said,

> *Take no thought for your life, what ye shall eat, or what ye shall drink; nor yet for your body, what ye shall put on. ...(For after all these things do the Gentiles seek:) for your heavenly Father knoweth that ye have need of all these things. But seek ye first the kingdom of God, and his righteousness; and all these things shall be added unto you. Take therefore no thought for the morrow: for the morrow shall take thought for the things of itself. Sufficient unto the day is the evil thereof.*
>
> MATTHEW 6:25,32-34

If the kingdom of God is inside of us, then we don't need to worry about anything. God has already provided everything.

Now we can understand the psalmist's words, "A thousand shall fall at thy side, and ten thousand at thy right hand; but it shall not come nigh thee" (Ps. 91:7). God's protection is one provision of the kingdom that is inside of us.

We can't see the kingdom; however, we can see the results of it. Jesus said, "The kingdom of God cometh not with observation: neither shall they say, Lo here! or, lo there! for the kingdom of God is within you" (Luke 17:20-21). The kingdom of God is a spiritual reality and is more real than anything we can see with our physical eyes.

When we receive Jesus, we receive it all. We have a spiritual fountain inside, and we will never thirst again (John 4:13). We will never have to go to another source to provide for us. Everything we need is inside of us. God will bring to us, lead us to, and create for us everything that we need in this earth, independent of what's going on around us.

WHAT WE HAVE IS FOR THE NATIONS

Jesus said, "He that believeth on me, as the scripture hath said, out of his belly shall flow rivers of living water" (John 7:38). The well is meant to provide water for us and our families, but the river is also meant to provide for the nations. As believers, we contain kingdom provisions to take care of the nations of the earth.

Not only do we have natural provision for the people of the world, but we have the supernatural provision they need as well. Though they may not realize it, they are enslaved to the kingdom of darkness. Through fear and deception, demons influence people to live in a way that is not consistent with the laws of God. Demonic spirits control the ungodly kingdoms of this world. However, when we receive Jesus, we receive His kingdom and evil spirits lose ground in this world.

As ambassadors for the King of kings, we have come into this foreign territory, not to take sides but to take over: to dominate this territory and make it like heaven. Jesus "went about doing good, and healing all that were oppressed of the devil; for God was with him" (Acts 10:38). Now He sends us to be its witness to show proof of the King and this new kingdom. We have to help them trust in a kingdom that they cannot see with their physical eyes.

If we want to be witnesses of the kingdom, we will have to see it and experience it for ourselves; then we will be able to demonstrate it. We need revelation, and we have to change our focus from this world to the kingdom of God.

HEAVEN'S TREASURE VS. MAMMON

Once we have the kingdom inside, the Holy Spirit's job is to help us to get the world out of us. Only then can we be in the world but not of the world. This requires a turning away from our own way and going God's way. We repented when we received Jesus Christ and His salvation; but as the Holy Spirit reveals to us that we have trusted the world's system and not God in certain areas, we will need to repent again.

We cannot serve two masters. We can't serve the world and Jesus. "For either he will hate the one, and love the other; or else he will hold to the one, and despise the other. Ye cannot serve God and mammon" (Matt. 6:24). People say they're serving Jesus, but they're holding on to the world's system. The world's system does not save souls, it saves money; it tells us to store up all our treasure here. But Jesus said:

> *Lay not up for yourselves treasures upon earth, where moth and rust doth corrupt, and where thieves break through and steal: but lay up for yourselves treasures in heaven, where neither moth nor rust doth corrupt, and*

where thieves do not break through nor steal: for where your treasure is, there will your heart be also.

The light of the body is the eye: if therefore thine eye be single, thy whole body shall be full of light. But if thine eye be evil, thy whole body shall be full of darkness. If therefore the light that is in thee be darkness, how great is that darkness! No man can serve two masters: for either he will hate the one, and love the other; or else he will hold to the one, and despise the other. Ye cannot serve God and mammon.

MATTHEW 6:19-24

This is the message Jesus wanted to convey to the rich young ruler who asked Him, "Good Master, what shall I do to inherit eternal life?" (Luke 18:18).

Jesus said, "Thou knowest the commandments, Do not commit adultery, Do not kill, Do not steal, Do not bear false witness, Honour thy father and thy mother" (v. 20). The rich young ruler replied confidently, "All these have I kept from my youth" (v. 21). He was religious, and he had been careful to do everything on the list.

But then Jesus said, "Yet lackest thou one thing: sell all that thou hast, and distribute unto the poor, and thou shalt have treasure in heaven: and come, follow me" (v. 22). Notice, He didn't say, "You're going to go broke." He said, in essence, "You'll have treasure on a higher plane, and that treasure is available when you need it."

When Jesus spoke to that rich young ruler, He was trying to show him who his real god was. His real god was not the Lord

29

God Jehovah. His real god was his money. If our money is telling us what to do, it is in effect our god or master.

When the rich young ruler heard Jesus say that the only thing he lacked was to sell "what you have and give to the poor" and follow Him, he bowed his head and walked away. He couldn't do that, because he thought he was going to suffer loss. He didn't have the full revelation of the kingdom of God because his focus was divided between the world system and God's kingdom.

Jesus said, "If therefore thine eye be single, thy whole body shall be full of light." If our intent is to depend on God and our eye is single, or our focus is entirely on God, then our body will be full of the revelation that it takes to live in the kingdom of God. However, if we try to look at God a little bit and try to hold on to the world's system because we're not sure if "this God thing" will work, then darkness will come in and we won't have the light of His Word guiding our lives. Like the rich young ruler, we'll think God is trying to take something from us or make us fall. We'll back up and walk away and say, "No, He won't take all this. I worked too hard for this."

However, with the revelation of the kingdom, we will see that we are living in two realms. We're living in the kingdom of God, and we're living in the realm of the natural, five physical senses. Only revelation knowledge can take you beyond your intellect and this natural physical matter. Without Jesus Christ, that sense realm is the boundary of life. However, once we become born again, we receive a new life—eternal life— which takes us beyond natural boundaries into the place where all things become possible.

Now all things are possible to us who believe. No other religion can offer this reality. Hear that again: No other "religion" can truthfully make this claim. However, the church has not been demonstrating this new reality, so people have been looking at the church the same way they look at any other religion. That will not be the case for long. We are entering a new day: a day when the church will receive revelation of the kingdom, manifest His Word, and reclaim the earth for the King.

CHAPTER 3

DANIEL'S VISION OF THE COMING KINGDOM

B efore we go any further, you may be having doubts about "reclaiming the earth for the King" and "taking our dominion." In the Old Testament book of Daniel, we find one of the clearest descriptions of the kingdom of God reclaiming the earth. The young Hebrew named Daniel actually describes a vision he had of the kingdom of God coming into the earth.

Daniel was a young man who, along with an elite group of young Judeans, was taken captive by the Babylonian king Nebuchadnezzar.

> *And the king spake unto Ashpenaz the master of his eunuchs, that he should bring certain of the children of Israel, and of the king's seed, and of the princes; children in whom was no blemish, but well favoured, and*

skilful in all wisdom, and cunning in knowledge, and understanding science, and such as had ability in them to stand in the king's palace, and whom they might teach the learning and the tongue of the Chaldeans.

DANIEL 1:3-4

Daniel and some of the Hebrews possessed gifts and talents from God's kingdom, and the Babylonians took notice. As a result, a worldly government took God's people captive.

While serving in Babylon, Daniel was presented with an opportunity to demonstrate revelation knowledge from God's kingdom. King Nebuchadnezzar had a dream that disturbed him, but he woke up the next morning and couldn't remember what he'd dreamed. He called in the magicians, the soothsayers, the wizards, the Chaldeans (the people of the world), and said, "You tell me what I dreamed and what that dream meant." However, the wisdom of the world couldn't do that, and Daniel 2:12-13 tells us how the king responded to their inability:

For this cause the king was angry and very furious, and commanded to destroy all the wise men of Babylon. And the decree went forth that the wise men should be slain; and they sought Daniel and his fellows to be slain.

Things didn't look very good for the wise men in Babylon, including Daniel and his fellow Hebrew captives. Daniel, knowing his life was on the line, responded by approaching the throne. "Could I see the king?" he said. "I can get the answer for him. I know my God knows what to do. He knows what the king dreamed."

THE KING'S DREAM

The king gave Daniel some time to seek God, and then we read in verses 19-23:

Then was the secret revealed unto Daniel in a night vision. Then Daniel blessed the God of heaven. Daniel answered and said, Blessed be the name of God for ever and ever: for wisdom and might are his: And he changeth the times and the seasons: he removeth kings, and setteth up kings: he giveth wisdom unto the wise, and knowledge to them that know understanding: He revealeth the deep and secret things: he knoweth what is in the darkness, and the light dwelleth with him. I thank thee, and praise thee, O thou God of my fathers, who hast given me wisdom and might, and hast made known unto me now what we desired of thee: for thou hast now made known unto us the king's matter.

God told Daniel the dream and its interpretation, and Daniel went in to meet the king. He said, "God has made known to me the dream" and began telling the king the dream and what it meant.

Thou, O king, sawest, and behold a great image. This great image, whose brightness was excellent, stood before thee; and the form thereof was terrible. This image's head was of fine gold, his breast and his arms of silver, his belly and his thighs of brass, his legs of iron, his feet part of iron and part of clay. Thou sawest till that a stone was cut out without hands, which smote the image upon his feet that were of iron and clay, and brake them to pieces. Then was the iron, the clay, the brass, the silver, and the gold, broken to pieces together, and became like the chaff of the summer threshing floors; and the wind carried them away, that no place was found for them: and the stone that smote the image became a great mountain, and filled the whole earth.

DANIEL 2:31-35

THE DREAM'S INTERPRETATION

Verses 37 through 45 contain the interpretation of this dream:

Thou, O king, art a king of kings: for the God of heaven hath given thee a kingdom, power, and strength, and glory. And wheresoever the children of men dwell, the beasts of the field and the fowls of the heaven hath he given into thine hand, and hath made thee ruler over them all. Thou art this head of gold. And after thee shall arise another kingdom inferior to thee, and another third kingdom of brass, which shall bear rule over all the earth.

And the fourth kingdom shall be strong as iron: forasmuch as iron breaketh in pieces and subdueth all things: and as iron that breaketh all these, shall it break in pieces and bruise.

And whereas thou sawest the feet and toes, part of potters' clay, and part of iron, the kingdom shall be divided; but there shall be in it of the strength of the iron, forasmuch as thou sawest the iron mixed with miry clay. And

*as the toes of the feet were part of iron, and part of clay,
so the kingdom shall be partly strong, and partly broken.
And whereas thou sawest iron mixed with miry clay,
they shall mingle themselves with the seed of men: but
they shall not cleave one to another, even as iron is not
mixed with clay.*

*And in the days of these kings shall the God of heaven
set up a kingdom, which shall never be destroyed: and
the kingdom shall not be left to other people, but it shall
break in pieces and consume all these kingdoms, and it
shall stand for ever. Forasmuch as thou sawest that the
stone was cut out of the mountain without hands, and
that it brake in pieces the iron, the brass, the clay, the
silver, and the gold; the great God hath made known
to the king what shall come to pass hereafter: and the
dream is certain, and the interpretation thereof sure.*

The picture represents the kingdoms that would rule in
this earth, each metal symbolizing the order and strength of
that particular world government. It also reveals that in the end
God's kingdom will enter the earth and overturn every government in the world.

THE GOLD HEAD: THE BABYLONIAN EMPIRE

*This image's **head was of fine gold.***

DANIEL 2:32 (bold mine)

The gold head represents the Babylonian kingdom, which
was a dictatorship, or authoritarian rule. The fact that this government of pure gold was the head of the worldly governments

implies that this is the closest thing the earth has to compare with the kingdom of God. The highest worldly kingdom represented in the dream is an authoritarian (dictatorship) type government in which one ruler rules the kingdom. The kingdom of God is a theocracy, not a democracy, because the One Lord is in charge.

In John 18:36, Jesus says, "My kingdom is not of this world." It's **His** kingdom, not ours, and He gives the decrees. He has the last word, and He is not confused or deceived. Jesus is a holy, righteous King. So the first and highest form of worldly government that Daniel saw in his vision, the gold head, was an authoritarian government.

SILVER BREAST AND ARMS: THE MEDO-PERSIAN EMPIRE

*This image's head was of fine gold, **his breast and his arms of silver**.*

DANIEL 2:32 (BOLD MINE)

The second worldly government in Daniel's vision is inferior to the first because it is illustrated by the image's silver breast and arms, and silver is inferior to gold. This part of the image represents the Medo-Persian Empire. This government took over while Daniel was still living in Babylon.

In that night was Belshazzar the king of the Chaldeans slain. And Darius the Median took the kingdom, being about threescore and two years old.

DANIEL 5:30-31

King Darius was sixty-two years old when he took over the Persian kingdom. The Medians joined forces with the Persians and began the Medo-Persian Empire.

> *It pleased Darius to set over the kingdom an hundred and twenty princes, which should be over the whole kingdom; and over these three presidents; of whom Daniel was first: that the princes might give accounts unto them, and the king should have no damage. Then this Daniel was preferred above the presidents and princes, because an excellent spirit was in him; and the king thought to set him over the whole realm.*
>
> DANIEL 6:1-3

Because Daniel was a Hebrew and was operating as a representative of the kingdom of God, King Darius favored him and planned to set him in high rule. However, the leaders of the worldly kingdom got jealous about it and set out to destroy Daniel.

> *Then the presidents and princes sought to find occasion against Daniel concerning the kingdom; but they could find none occasion nor fault; forasmuch as he was faithful, neither was there any error or fault found in him. Then said these men, We shall not find any occasion against this Daniel, except we find it against him concerning the law of his God.*
>
> DANIEL 6:4-5

These worldly rulers wanted to find some fault with Daniel, but the only way they could was to persuade the king to make a law against the law of God.

This is one way that the enemy has tried the church. He has caused the world's governments to make legislation that promotes their evil agendas and is opposed to the kingdom of God.

Then these presidents and princes assembled together to the king, and said thus unto him, King Darius, live for ever. All the presidents of the kingdom, the governors, and the princes, the counsellors, and the captains, have consulted together to establish a royal statute, and to make a firm decree, that whosoever shall ask a petition of any God or man for thirty days, save of thee, O king, he shall be cast into the den of lions. Now, O king, establish the decree, and sign the writing, that it be not changed, according to the law of the Medes and Persians, which altereth not.

DANIEL 6:6-8

The Medo-Persian Empire governed according to the rule of law, which meant that when the king signed a decree in writing it could not be changed. The silver breast and arms in Daniel's vision represents this rule of law, or simply the law ruling over people rather than people ruling over people.

The leaders came together with one voice to advise the king, and he made the law.

Wherefore King Darius signed the writing and the decree. Now when Daniel knew that the writing was signed, he went into his house; and his windows being

> *open in his chamber toward Jerusalem, he kneeled upon*
> *his knees three times a day, and prayed, and gave thanks*
> *before his God, as he did aforetime.*
>
> DANIEL 6:9,10

If there ever is a worldly law that challenges the law of God, we must do as Daniel did and follow the law of God. Daniel wasn't intimidated by these people coming together and making a law that would require him to violate his God. He wasn't going to do that. When Daniel knew that the writing was signed he went into his house, left the windows opened, "kneeled upon his knees three times a day and prayed, and gave thanks before his God."

Of course, he was discovered and, although King Darius was upset and worked diligently to save Daniel from entering the lions' den, the written law could not be changed. In the end Daniel was thrown into the lions' den, but the lions couldn't eat him because he was under the authority of a more powerful government, the kingdom of God, and God protected him.

BRASS BELLY AND THIGHS: THE GREEK EMPIRE

> *This image's head was of fine gold, his breast and his arms of silver,* ***his belly and his thighs of brass.***
>
> DANIEL 2:32 (bold mine)

After the gold head and the silver breast and arms, Daniel saw in this vision the image's brass belly and thighs. Brass is inferior to silver and gold. The brass belly and thighs represent the Greek Empire. Alexander the Great set out to make the whole world Greek, but his efforts were cut short when he died at the age of thirty-three. His Grecian kingdom championed free thinking. They believed that whatever a person thought was right was truly right.

During his reign Alexander made Greek the language of the educated and the language of the masses in the great centers of commerce throughout the civilized world. In this atmosphere of "free thinking" emerged philosophers such as Socrates and Plato. Everyone was considered to be right, and there was no clear distinction between good and evil.[1] Today we have philosophies such as Relativism. Relativists believe that each individual's perception of truth is dependent upon their culture and experience.[2] In other words, there is no absolute truth, nor is there a God who establishes absolute truth. Everything is relative.

The Greeks also championed certain disciplines over others—disciplines such as academics, physical strength, trade, and business. Elsewhere, and even today, people respect all of these disciplines. In many cultures, whether a person is strong in a trade, in a sport, or in academia, that person is respected and can earn a place at the top of their discipline. In some countries and especially in the West, if a person receives poor marks in school or doesn't attend a fine college or university, it's almost as if that person is in a lesser class. However, that's not the way God sees it. The Bible says He is no respecter of persons, and He has chosen the foolish things of the world to confound the wise (Acts 10:34; 1 Cor. 1:27).

This third worldly government, like the first two, was overpowered by the next worldly government and would one day have to bow to God's infinitely superior kingdom.

IRON LEGS: THE ROMAN EMPIRE

*This image's head was of fine gold, his breast and his arms of silver, his belly and his thighs of brass, **his legs of iron**.*

DANIEL 2:32-33 (bold mine)

The legs of iron represent the strong Roman Empire, and as we know, iron is inferior to gold, silver, and brass. Rome's system of government was similar to a democracy because more than one person made the decisions. The Romans had a senate and an emperor, much like the Senate and president we now have in the United States. Americans generally believe our system of government is superior to any other system of government. However, it is interesting to note that this democratic form of government is next to the last and lowest of all the worldly kingdoms in Daniel's vision.

IRON AND CLAY FEET: THE DIVIDED ROMAN EMPIRE

*This image's head was of fine gold, his breast and his arms of silver, his belly and his thighs of brass, his legs of iron, **his feet part of iron and part of clay**.*

DANIEL 2:32-33 (bold mine)

The strong Roman Empire would eventually divide. Daniel 2:41 prophesied, "And whereas thou sawest the feet and toes, part of potters' clay, and part of iron, the kingdom shall be divided; but there shall be in it of the strength of the iron, forasmuch as thou sawest the iron mixed with miry clay." The

Roman Empire was overtaken by ten European nations, each of which took a piece of it.

Daniel 2:43 says, "And whereas thou sawest iron mixed with miry clay, they shall mingle themselves with the seed of men: but they shall not cleave one to another, even as iron is not mixed with clay." These nations would never unify, though they would try—and they are still trying today in the form of the European Union.

A SUPERNATURAL SYSTEM BREAKS THROUGH

Finally, in verses 34-35 we find a whole new system breaking through every form of worldly government:

> *Thou sawest till that a stone was cut out without hands, which smote the image upon his feet that were of iron and clay, and brake them to pieces. Then was the iron, the clay, the brass, the silver, and the gold, broken to pieces together, and became like the chaff of the summer threshingfloors; and the wind carried them away, that no place was found for them: and the stone that smote the image became a great mountain, and filled the whole earth.*

The stone cut without hands was the stone that the builders rejected (Ps. 118:22; Matt. 21:42). That stone is Jesus Christ, who represents God's messianic kingdom. The dream prophecies that the kingdoms of this world will be replaced by the kingdom of God, as also prophesied in the book of Revelation.

The dominion (kingdom, sovereignty, rule) of the world has now come into the possession and become the kingdom of our Lord and of His Christ (the Messiah), and He shall reign forever and ever (for eternities of the eternities)!

REVELATION 11:15 AMP

Isaiah prophesied that this kingdom would spread throughout the earth, and would increase without end.

For unto us a child is born, unto us a son is given: and the government shall be upon his shoulder: and his name shall be called Wonderful, Counsellor, The mighty God, The everlasting Father, The Prince of Peace. Of the increase of his government and peace there shall be no end, upon the throne of David, and upon his kingdom, to order it, and to establish it with judgment and with justice from henceforth even for ever. The zeal of the Lord of hosts will perform this.

ISAIAH 9:6-7

Jesus came to bring the government of God back into the earth to rule over all. And Daniel's prophetic vision also makes it clear that the kingdom of God has come to take over the kingdoms of this world. Today, as citizens of the kingdom of God, we are to move forward in Jesus Christ as the stone who increased into a mountain and covered the whole earth.

CHAPTER 4

RECLAIMING THE EARTH

If we are to reclaim the earth, then we need to first understand that the supernatural is the foundation for all things, but the natural realm became predominant in human life when Adam and Eve fell. At that moment, the Bible says, their eyes were opened (Gen. 3:7). They became self-conscious rather than God-conscious. They became sense-oriented instead of Spirit-led. They became limited to information in their minds rather than revelation in their hearts.

Before the Fall Adam and Eve operated at a completely different level in every area. They were at a higher level of understanding, victory, joy, prosperity, peace, and power. They experienced a higher level of knowledge called revelation knowledge. Everything was super. Even they were super. When Jesus came into the earth, He came as the last Adam and demonstrated where Adam and Eve operated before the Fall. He came preaching the kingdom of God: the kingdom that we live in when we are born again; the kingdom that comes not only in word but with enough power to bring itself to pass; the kingdom that will produce more than enough for us. Jesus preached both the kingdom and salvation.

There are two aspects of the gospel. The gospel of Jesus Christ is the gospel that brings a person to salvation. The gospel of the kingdom is the gospel that unhooks the person from the world's system. The gospel of the kingdom is instruction in God's Word to depend on and serve God and not this world. The gospel of the kingdom is the gospel Jesus preached about and teaches us about. It's a new order of living by faith.

As Christ's body, we need a revelation of this kingdom life. We are made to operate on the same supernatural level that Adam and Eve operated on before the Fall. We are made to live in a kingdom that produces more than enough for us. To get there, we will need revelation of the kingdom.

MADE TO FUNCTION LIKE GOD

Genesis 1:26 says,

> *And God said, Let us make man in our image, after our likeness: and let them have dominion over the fish of the sea, and over the fowl of the air, and over the cattle, and over all the earth, and over every creeping thing that creepeth upon the earth.*

God made us to function just like Him in the earth. He gave us dominion, which means rule and lordship, over all the earth.

He made us to govern and manage the earth and its resources in the very beginning.

Verse 27 says,

> *So God created man in his own image, in the image of God created he him; male and female created he them.*

God created humans in His image and in His class, as under-rulers in the earth. Humans didn't create God. The created will never be God. We will never be El Shaddai, God Almighty, yet God gave us authority and responsibility over the earth's resources.

> *And God blessed them and said to them, Be fruitful, multiply, and fill the earth, and subdue it [using all its vast resources in the service of God and man]; and have dominion over the fish of the sea, the birds of the air, and over every living creature that moves upon the earth.*
>
> GENESIS 1:28 AMP

God placed in the earth vast resources, such as water, animals, wood, and gold. Then He gave Adam and Eve dominion and authority over everything that He put in the earth. He told them to subdue it. We can infer, then, that God was saying, "I'm not going to subdue the earth for you; you're going to subdue it because it is under you." Psalm 115:16 confirms this, saying,

> *The heaven, even the heavens, are the Lord's: but the earth hath he given to the children of men.*

God intended this earth to be ours. We were supposed to rule it and subdue it. However, we can't do anything without Him. Adam and Eve discovered this when they sinned and became separated from Him.

ADAM AND EVE BOWED TO THE DEVIL

God entrusted all of the earth's resources to Adam and Eve when He told them to subdue it, be fruitful, and multiply. God and mankind worked together on the earth for a while, and everything was super. But then they bowed their knee to Satan, and their sin separated them from God and put them under the spiritual authority of God's enemy.

Ephesians 2:1-6 says,

> *And you hath he quickened, who were dead in trespasses and sins; wherein in time past ye walked according to the course of this world, according to the prince of the power of the air, the spirit that now worketh in the children of disobedience: among whom also we all had our conversation in times past in the lusts of our flesh, fulfilling the desires of the flesh and of the mind; and were by nature the children of wrath, even as others. But God, who is rich in mercy, for his great love wherewith he loved us, even when we were dead in sins, hath quickened us together with Christ, (by grace ye are saved;) and hath raised us up together, and made us sit together in heavenly places in Christ Jesus.*

Everyone in the world was once in the category of disobedient people under the control of demon spirits. However, by grace Jesus Christ has "raised us up together, and made us sit together in heavenly places in Christ Jesus."

First John 5:19 says, "And we know that we are of God, and the whole world lieth in wickedness." Everyone in the world who has not been born into the kingdom of God is under the deception of Satan, whom Revelation 12:9 refers to as "that old serpent called the devil and Satan, which deceiveth the whole world." Satan deceived all of us.

JESUS DEFEATED THE DEVIL

When Jesus died, He paid the price for every person's sin and gave each of us a way back to God. When He rose again, He defeated the devil in open combat and stripped from him all the spiritual authority that he had over Adam. From the time of the Fall, Satan had held mankind in bondage to consequences of their sin, which was death and hell.

Speaking of Jesus, Hebrews 2:14-15 explains how He became a man to defeat the devil and free us all from his death grip on our lives.

> *Forasmuch then as the children are partakers of flesh and blood, he also himself likewise took part of the same; that through death he might destroy him that had the power of death, that is, the devil; And deliver them who through fear of death were all their lifetime subject to bondage.*

Jesus said,

*I am he that liveth, and was dead; and, behold, I am
alive for evermore, Amen; and have the keys of hell and
of death.*

REVELATION 1:18

The keys of hell and of death are now in Jesus' hands! That
means that through Him we can be free of Satan's spiritual
authority, be reconciled to God, and live under God's spiritual
authority. Instead of walking in fear of death and hell, we walk
in faith and the confidence of everlasting life in Him. Now the
only keys we are concerned with are the keys of the kingdom of
God that Jesus gives us when we are born again.

WE HAVE THE KEYS OF THE KINGDOM

Jesus has given us the keys of the kingdom. Now we take
these keys, and whatever we bind on earth is bound in heaven.
Whatever we loose on earth is loosed in heaven.

*And I will give unto thee the keys of the kingdom of
heaven: and whatsoever thou shalt bind on earth shall
be bound in heaven: and whatsoever thou shalt loose on
earth shall be loosed in heaven.*

MATTHEW 16:19

As believers and children of God, we now have authority in
His name to storm the gates of hell. We can speak things that
be not as though they were, and all heaven backs us up (Rom.
4:17). In His name, we can cast out devils. In His name, we can
lay hands on the sick and they will recover (Mark 16:17,18). In
His name, we can call resources in—we can speak to a mountain and it will be removed (Mark 11:23.)

Jesus restored us to God, and when we operate in the authority of the name of Jesus, every resource in this earth becomes subject once again to the kingdom of God. Every place we set foot becomes holy ground, and Satan and the disobedient who are following his influence are defeated.

Jesus has legally restored us to our Father God and given us His authority, the authority of His name. Furthermore, as children of His kingdom, all the riches of God and heaven are ours. However, we have to know how the kingdom of God works in order to access what He has given us.

RISING TO A HIGHER LEVEL

As we receive revelation of the gospel of the kingdom, we will rise to a higher level in every area of our lives. The standards of this world and its system are much below the standards of heaven. In the economic system in the earth, for example, when we invest money we expect to receive interest back. One hundred percent interest, or doubling an investment, would be a great return. However, in the kingdom of God we're able to bank on another level. We're able to sow a seed and receive a thirty-, sixty-, or hundredfold return.

The kingdom of God is on a completely different level than this world's system. To live in it, we will have to live from the inside out, not the outside in. We were never intended to live out of our mind and flesh; we were intended to live out of our spirit.

The spirit is the part of us that will receive revelation of the kingdom. Proverbs 20:27 says, "The spirit of man is the candle of the Lord, searching all the inward parts of the belly." God guides us through our spirit, not our mind. Psalm 18:28 refers to the spirit as a candle, saying, "For thou will light my candle, the Lord my God will enlighten my darkness." God's revelation will bring light where there has been darkness in our lives.

We were made to operate on a higher plane than just head knowledge. We were made to live by revelation in our heart, by the Lord lighting our candle (spirit) and enlightening our darkness (understanding). When we do, we can see what the world can't see—the kingdom of God. We won't go the way of the world, and we won't be conformed to it because we are operating according to the Spirit and not the flesh.

WE NEED THE KNOWLEDGE OF GOD

If we don't have the knowledge of God, we cannot come out of the world's system and into the kingdom reality. Second Peter 1:2-4 says,

> *Grace and peace be multiplied unto you through the knowledge of God, and of Jesus our Lord, according as his divine power hath given unto us all things that pertain unto life and godliness, through the knowledge of him that hath called us to glory and virtue: whereby are given unto us exceeding great and precious promises: that by these ye might be partakers of the divine nature.*

The knowledge of God is revelation knowledge. It's not natural knowledge, and it is through this knowledge that we obtain the great and precious promises of God's kingdom. In Hosea 4:6, God says, "My people are destroyed for lack of knowledge." He didn't say, "My people are destroyed for lack of money" or "education," but they're destroyed "for lack of [revelation] knowledge."

Real wealth doesn't come by education; it comes by revelation. Thank God for education, but if that's all we have we're in trouble. An economic earthquake is coming, and education won't save us. If we want to make it through, we'll need revelation of how to stand on the Rock and how to receive our provision directly from Almighty God.

This is why the kingdom of God must be preached. The kingdom of God is God's way of doing things, and it comes with provision. Through His kingdom, God has given us everything that we will ever need, independent of what happens in this world.

In the last days, there will be diseases that won't have a medical cure. The only place we'll be able to find a cure is in the Word of God. Jesus said His disciples would lay hands on the sick in His name and they would recover (Mark 16:18). We are His disciples, the church; the kingdom is in us. We can go out and take healing to the world—to the job, to the health club, to the beauty shop—everywhere we go. God's kingdom power is wherever we are.

We're supposed to be opening up the drug houses and restoring people to wholeness in the name of Jesus. We have something that will turn them in another direction and satisfy them so that they never need to take another drug. We have something more powerful than the drugs they have. We have the Holy Spirit.

First Corinthians 2:12-13 says,

> *Now we have received, not the spirit of the world, but the spirit which is of God; that we might know the things that are freely given to us of God. Which things*

also we speak, not in the words which man's wisdom teacheth, but which the Holy Ghost teacheth; comparing spiritual things with spiritual.

The only One who can teach us is the Holy Spirit, and we can only understand His teaching by the spirit.

First Corinthians 2:14 says,

But the natural man receiveth not the things of the Spirit of God: for they are foolishness unto him: neither can he know them, because they are spiritually discerned.

The kingdom remains a mystery to people who really don't want it. People who don't plan to go to God won't even see the kingdom. However, the people who have a heart for God and want to know more about Him and want to serve Him will see something that the world can't see.

REVELATION COMES FROM THE FATHER

Jesus said to His disciples, "Whom do men say that I the Son of man am?" (Matt. 16:13).

Some replied, "Some say that thou art John the Baptist: some, Elias; and others, Jeremias, or one of the prophets" (v. 14).

He said, "But whom say ye that I am?" (v. 15). Simon Peter said, "Thou art the Christ, the Son of the living God" (v. 16).

Jesus replied,

Blessed art thou, Simon Barjona: for flesh and blood hath not revealed it unto thee, but my Father which is in heaven. And I say also unto thee, That thou art

Peter, and upon this rock I will build my church; and the gates of hell shall not prevail against it.

MATTHEW 16:17,18

Simon was flaky, but Peter was a rock. He went from being flaky to being solid because of what he could see. The reason the gates of hell couldn't prevail against Peter was that now he could see the kingdom. He had the light. He had the revelation.

Notice that it was the Father who revealed who Jesus was. In the mystery of the kingdom, God has reserved these truths for those seeking after Him. People who are not in the kingdom of God yet, but are seeking, may hear God's voice but don't really know what He is saying or what to do when they hear it.

Even most believers don't have this revelation because their hearts are not set to depend on God. They're still locked into this world, depending on this world as their source. God says, "I don't want the world to be your source. I want you to be locked into Me. You're under a new government with a new King, who wants to take care of you."

I don't want you to close this book, jump up, and call your boss to quit your job because Jesus is going to take care of you now. However, if God asked you to do just that and gave you revelation of where you should go and what you should do, your faith would rise up at His word and there would be no risk. This way of life is normal to citizens of God's kingdom, but strange to those in the world.

ODD TO THE WORLD

When we live by the revelation of the kingdom of God, sometimes we will seem odd to the world. We have to stop comparing ourselves with the world and trying to get along by hiding our heavenly citizenship.

The Bible says we are a peculiar people, a royal priesthood (1 Pet. 2:9). God knew we were different when He called us here. When everybody in the world is crying, we ought to be rejoicing. When everyone is talking about terrorism and saying they won't fly in an airplane, we should be saying, "Well, I guess I'll be on it by myself!" Something should be different about kingdom citizens. We should be living a different lifestyle. We have to stop conforming to the world. We've got to stop living on the level of the world and start letting the kingdom provide what we need. Ephesians 1:3 says, "Blessed be the God and Father of our Lord Jesus Christ, who hath blessed us with all spiritual blessings in heavenly places in Christ." It's already done, and it's in the kingdom for us.

When we receive the revelation of the kingdom of God, we will take back all of the earth's resources and live as God created us to live. We will take the kingdom by force.

CHAPTER 5

TAKING THE
KINGDOM BY FORCE

Jesus lived the kingdom life and was our example in this earth. He came to the earth to die for humankind, to bring us back into union with God. He came because Adam and Eve sinned and separated all of humanity from the kingdom of God. Jesus demonstrated that the kingdom of God rules over everything, and He taught us that the violent take the kingdom by force.

> *The kingdom of heaven has endured violent assault, and violent men seize it by force [as a precious prize— a share in the heavenly kingdom is sought with most ardent zeal and intense exertion].*
> MATTHEW 11:12 AMP

Then He taught us to pray, "Thy kingdom come, Thy will be done in earth, as it is in heaven" (Matt. 6:10). Satan trembled at Jesus' ministry, and he tried to tempt Him to keep Him from going forward, exposing his demonic system, and establishing God's kingdom in this earth. However, Jesus defeated him on every turn, and He has enabled us to do the same.

THE DEVIL TEMPTED JESUS

And the devil said unto him, If thou be the Son of God, command this stone that it be made bread.

LUKE 4:3

At this point in time, Jesus had just fasted forty days and was hungry. His body was demanding food. Nevertheless, to Satan's temptation Jesus said, "It is written, That man shall not live by bread alone, but by every word of God." Bread is for the natural man; the Word of God is for the spiritual man. Believers need both to live victoriously on this earth.

Luke 4:5-6 records how the devil responded.

And the devil, taking him up into an high mountain, shewed unto him all the kingdoms of the world in a moment of time. And the devil said unto him, All this power will I give thee, and the glory of them: for that is delivered unto me; and to whomsoever I will I give it.

Adam and Eve had delivered the kingdom of God and their power and glory to the devil, and he had used disobedient humankind to build his kingdom. His kingdom and systems imitate God's. His kingdom is not the real thing; it's a fake, a counterfeit. And just as God's kingdom comes with demonstration of His supernatural power, Satan's system comes with counterfeit signs and wonders.

> *And then shall that Wicked be revealed, whom the Lord shall consume with the spirit of his mouth, and shall destroy with the brightness of his coming: even him, whose coming is after the working of Satan with all power and signs and lying wonders, and with all deceivableness of unrighteousness in them that perish; because they received not the love of the truth, that they might be saved.*
>
> 2 THESSALONIANS 2:8-10

Satan has lying signs and wonders. They're really not the truth; they're based on deception.

Satan even deceives people who think they are working for God. For example, Saul of Tarsus (who became Paul the apostle) thought he was doing right by crucifying Christians and sending them to jail (Acts 8-9). He was just as wrong as two left shoes, but he was deceived. Likewise, Eve was deceived. She thought she was doing right when she ate the fruit from the tree of the knowledge of good and evil, but she was absolutely wrong (Gen. 3.)

We don't have to be deceived. Revelation 12:9 says that the devil deceives the whole world, but it doesn't say that he deceives the church. We have a higher knowledge inside, the knowledge of God. And when we tap into the knowledge of God we will not be deceived.

Revelation 18:23 says, "By thy sorceries were all nations deceived," and Galatians 5:19-20 says that witchcraft is the work of the flesh. However, verse 25 gives us the key to overcoming deception and the works of the flesh: "If we live in the Spirit, let us also walk in the Spirit."

As God's people, we must be led by the Spirit, and He will always lead us to the Living Word (John 14:26, 15:26). Then when the devil comes to tempt us as he did Jesus, we will also defeat him at every turn with the Word of God.

CONDEMN THE CURSE

When a person speaks a curse over someone's life, that curse gives demons license to go into the person's life and cause affliction and oppression. However, as children of God, we have dominion over the power of the enemy. Luke 10:17-19 says,

> *And the seventy returned again with joy, saying, Lord, even the devils are subject unto us through thy name. And he said unto them, I beheld Satan as lightning fall from heaven. Behold, I give unto you power to tread on serpents and scorpions, and over all the power of the enemy: and nothing shall by any means hurt you.*

Furthermore, Isaiah 54:17 says,

> *No weapon that is formed against thee shall prosper; and every tongue that shall rise against thee in judgment thou shalt condemn. This is the heritage of the servants of the Lord, and their righteousness is of me, saith the Lord.*

Remember: a curse is a work of the flesh. If the doctor says you have cancer and have six months to live, you say, "Doc, I know you believe what you say, but I have another report." Cut off the bad report and condemn the judgment against you by declaring the truth of God's Word.

Goliath cursed David by his gods (1 Sam. 17:43). Demons then were licensed to go after David, but David cut off Goliath's curse. David said, "Thou comest to me with a sword, and with a spear, and with a shield: but I come to thee in the name of the Lord of hosts, the God of the armies of Israel, whom thou hast defied" (v. 45).

When we call Jesus' name, every demon trembles. When we call Jesus' name, every angel stands at attention. We can cut off the curse in Jesus' name and by declaring His Word. When the doctor gives us a bad report, we can say, "I cancel that in the name of Jesus. By His stripes, I'm healed" (1 Pet. 2:24).

CALLED INTO KINGDOM LIVING

The world's system is under a curse, because it is under Satan's deceptive rule. The whole world is being oppressed, and Satan has been controlling the masses through sorcery, which is designed to put pressure on the minds of unbelievers (Eph. 2:2). But prayer in the name of Jesus will break the power of demon spirits operating over and controlling the masses.

For our prayer to be effective, however, we must live independent of the world's system and live the kingdom life. In my own life, God dealt with me about separating from the world's system and living according to the kingdom of God when He called me into full-time ministry.

When the Holy Spirit prompted me to leave the computer company that had been good to me, I tried several times to obey Him. However, every time I thought about it, the bills called me back. The house note, the car note, the new pair of shoes for the baby—everything in the world kept telling me I just couldn't leave.

But then I caught hold of this passage of Scripture:

> *And [Jesus] said unto them, Verily I say unto you, There is no man that hath left house, or parents, or brethren, or wife, or children, for the kingdom of God's sake, who shall not receive manifold more in this present time, and in the world to come life everlasting.*
>
> Luke 18:29-30

I began to meditate on this, and light began to come in. I began to look at God, not my job, as my source. The job had been good to me, but now it was time for me to separate from this world's system because "no man can serve two masters" (Matt. 6:24.)

One day I finally had the revelation of this truth, and I went to the boss and said, "Hey, I'm leaving the company."

He jumped up and closed the door and asked, "What's wrong?" I said, "Nothing's wrong."

The economy was bad right then. When I told my coworkers I was leaving, they said, "Oh, no. Don't leave now."

However, those people didn't have revelation knowledge, the light of God's kingdom. Light isn't information. If you only have information, you're still in darkness. **Light is revelation.** I had the light, and I could see the kingdom provisions ready for me.

The way that the enemy keeps his advantage over those he deceives is to keep them in darkness. Darkness means no light, no revelation of God. That's why we must be born again—translated from darkness to light. **Only when we are born again can we see the kingdom of God.** John 3:1-3 says,

> *There was a man of the Pharisees, named Nicodemus, a ruler of the Jews: the same came to Jesus by night, and said unto him, Rabbi, we know that thou art a teacher come from God: for no man can do these miracles that thou doest, except God be with him. Jesus answered and said unto him, Verily, verily, I say unto thee, Except a man be born again, he cannot see the kingdom of God.*

The kingdom of God is a mystery because we can't see it with our physical eyes. To flesh and blood, it's an unseen kingdom. But to those of us who are born again and walking in the Spirit and not the flesh, it is not only real; **it is extremely effective, powerful, and extravagant. Everything we need is in the kingdom of God.** When I saw this, I was able to quit my job with confidence and in faith.

GETTING THE WORLD OUT OF US

Jesus took us out of the world; now we need to get the world out of us. We have been saved but still need to be sanctified. First Corinthians 2:12-14 says,

> *Now we have received, not the spirit of the world, but the spirit which is of God; that we might know the things that are freely given to us of God. Which things*

also we speak, not in the words which man's wisdom teacheth, but which the Holy Ghost teacheth; comparing spiritual things with spiritual. But the natural man receiveth not the things of the Spirit of God: for they are foolishness unto him: neither can he know them, because they are spiritually discerned.

The things that we do and say are foolish to the natural part of us and to natural people. When we live from the spirit, our way of thinking and acting will seem strange to the world—and strange to us for a while. That's because we are getting used to the fact that we are in the world but not of it.

The more truth we receive and act on, the more separate we will become from the world and the more "natural" it will be to us. We can't separate from the world and live holy lives without the truth. Jesus prayed, "Sanctify them through thy truth: thy word is truth" (John 17:17). To be sanctified, we have to hear and do the Word.

When we're separating ourselves from the world's system, it's a fight—but we're going to win if we just persevere according to the truth that's in us. **We are far bigger on the inside than we are on the outside.** What God gives us to do is too big for our flesh and mind, but it's not too big for our spirit.

When Abraham asked God for a child, God said, "Look up. What do you see?" Abraham said, "Stars."

God said, "That's how many kids you're going to have." (See Genesis. 22:17.) Abraham's mind must have fought him all the way, but his spirit believed, and when he believed, his faith obtained the promise.

We come into the kingdom of God with a world-programmed mind. Then the first time God asks us to do something that has some vision, we tend to say, "I can't do that." We don't even know what we can do, but if we dig into the Word we'll find out! We have to take the kingdom by force: We have to dominate our flesh by our spirit by trusting in God's Word more than our own thinking.

LED BY THE SPIRIT

Galatians 5:18-21 says,

> *But if ye be led of the Spirit, ye are not under the law. Now the works of the flesh are manifest, which are these; Adultery, fornication, uncleanness, lasciviousness, idolatry, witchcraft, hatred, variance, emulations, wrath, strife, seditions, heresies, envyings, murders, drunkenness, revellings, and such like: of the which I tell you before, as I have also told you in time past, that they which do such things shall not inherit the kingdom of God.*

To make it plain, idolatry is thinking more about the ball game (or anything on earth) than we think about God. Then it leads to all the sinful things listed above. Those who do these things will not inherit the kingdom of God. That does not necessarily mean they are not saved. After all, the book of Galatians is written to saved people. It simply means they will not appropriate their inheritance in the kingdom of God.

We appropriate our inheritance in the kingdom of God by being led by the Spirit and not our flesh. And, as we saw earlier, the Holy Spirit will always lead us to God's Word. When we think, speak, and act in agreement with God's Word, we won't fall into idolatry and sin and lose our inheritance. Of course, when we start speaking the Word, some people will wonder what we're talking about. When rent is due, we'll be saying, "I have abundance and no lack." The kingdom way is to call things that be not as though they were (Rom. 4:17). We may not have the money in our hand at the moment, but we do have it in heaven right now. God has it there for us, and we just need to transfer it into the earth by speaking His Word.

We don't lack anything in God's kingdom. We have everything we need right now. God is eternal God; He's not a future God.

> *But, beloved, be not ignorant of this one thing, that one*
> *day is with the Lord as a thousand years, and a thou-*
> *sand years as one day.*
>
> 2 PETER 3:8

God created time and sits outside of time, so His concept of time is different from ours. We live in time, but God is the eternal now. When Moses asked God, "Who shall I say sent me?" God said, "Tell them I AM sent you." He didn't say, "Tell them 'I'm going to be' sent you" (Ex. 3:13,14). There is no future tense with God. Every promise in His Word is for us and is available now. God has already given us all things that pertain to life and godliness through the knowledge of Him, which we gain from His Word, His "exceeding great and precious promises."

> *His divine power hath given unto us all things that*
> *pertain unto life and godliness, through the knowledge*

of him that hath called us to glory and virtue: whereby
are given unto us exceeding great and precious promises:
that by these ye might be partakers of the divine nature.

2 PETER 1:3-4

God has already provided everything we need, and as members of the kingdom of God we can receive it now by our words. We receive our inheritance when we are led by the Spirit and speak God's Word into every situation.

THE WORD IN OUR MOUTH

Romans 10:8 says, "The word is nigh thee, even in thy mouth, and in thy heart." The word *heart* here doesn't refer to the blood pump; it refers to the real us, our spirit. When God gives us a word, it goes first in our mouth and then in our heart.

Verse 10 says, "For with the heart man believeth unto righteousness." Notice it doesn't say, "For with the head man believeth." We don't believe with our head; we believe with our heart. With our heart we believe unto righteousness. "And with the mouth confession is made unto salvation." The same goes for healing, prosperity, a good marriage, deliverance, and every victory we need. We receive all we need by confessing the gospel of the kingdom with our mouth and believing it in our heart.

As citizens of the kingdom of God, we can get some seed out of the Word of God, put it in our mouth to speak it, and it will go into our heart. Then that seed will produce what we need in our lives as God's ambassadors in the earth.

The reason speaking is so powerful is that it releases spiritual power from our hearts. We have something in us that is so powerful. God wants to do some things through us, but we can't look at the situation in terms of our flesh. God didn't call our flesh. He called us Spirit to spirit. God didn't tell our flesh to go into all the world. He told us, His spiritual children, to go into all the world and speak and do His Word.

THE POWER OF GOD'S WORD

Before light was in the earth, it was in God's words.

And God said, Let there be light: and there was light.
GENESIS 1:3

Not only are God's words powerful when spoken from His mouth, but He has empowered the words of our mouths as well. In Genesis 1:26 we find that He said, "Let us make man in our image, after our likeness." When He said this, He wasn't talking about our flesh because God is a spirit being. Our flesh is not us; it houses us. We are who we are inside, and there—in our spirit—we are the image and likeness of God's kind of being.

Jesus said that the Word of God is seed. The Bible says we were "born again, not of corruptible seed, but of incorruptible, by the word of God, which liveth and abideth for ever" (1 Pet. 1:23). We were born into the kingdom by the perfect seed of the Word of God. According to John 1:1, that seed of the Word is God Himself:

In the beginning was the Word, and the Word was with God, and the Word was God.

We are born of God, and every seed produces after its own kind. An apple seed produces an apple, a cow produces a cow, a horse produces a horse. The Word was God and the Word is seed, and we were born by that seed. Therefore, we were made like God. He placed in us what He has inside Himself. We are His children. He communicates with us, and He works with us to make Himself manifest in this earth.

WE ARE THE KINGDOM

The kingdom has come, and we are the kingdom. The kingdom government is the church. God is taking down the barriers within the church because He wants one family representing Him in the earth.

People have said, "Come to church with us," but that builds the wrong image. We're not *going* to church. We *are* the Church! Jesus said to Peter, "Thou art Peter, and upon this rock I will build my church; and the gates of hell shall not prevail against it" (Matt. 16:18). The truth is that when Jesus said, "Build My church," *My church* meant His people. *My church* is not a building. *My church* could meet down the street in the bar. Just cover up the liquor, and let's have some church!

We have brought people to the church building to get everything: to get saved, to get healed, and so forth. But the kingdom is in us to take salvation, healing, and every heavenly provision to the world. We don't have to bring the people to the church building. We can go to them.

If we're business people, our businesses should be an example of the kingdom. If we're healthcare workers, we should be the ones saying, "Let me pray for you." If we're in the school systems, we should be praying and receiving the wisdom of God to raise up our students to perform above standards. If we're married, our marriages should be an example of heaven for our neighbors to see.

No matter where we go, we take the kingdom with us. Jesus ate with tax collectors and sinners. Think about it. God so loved *the world* that He gave His only Son (John 3:16). He loved them. I don't know whom you don't like, but God loves them.

When we limit the kingdom of God to the inside of the four walls of the church building, psychologically the world becomes our adversary. Anyone outside of the walls becomes the enemy. Then all the churchgoers want to work for the church because they don't think they're supposed to be at that "secular" job. However, that secular job becomes subjugated to the kingdom of God the moment we step into it! It is exactly where many of us are supposed to be. We're supposed to take the kingdom with us into the world in which we work and live.

The enemy intentionally planted the idea in our minds that the church is limited to a building because he doesn't want us out in the harvest. He wants us to be afraid of it.

The devil also doesn't want us to know that the manifestation of God's kingdom—the blessing—comes from within us. He doesn't want us to know that we have enough kingdom of God in us to pray for our neighbor's healing over the back fence and see him recover. He doesn't want us to pull from the anointing inside of us for our coworker's migraine headache to clear up. He doesn't want us to go up to the drug house, open the door, and say, "Hey, I'm here, and I brought Somebody with me." He doesn't want us pulling the prostitute off the street and into the kingdom.

The enemy has talked us out of our harvest by containing us in the church walls and getting us to believe that that's the only place where God's power can operate. We've been scared to go out into the world, even scared to admit that we are Christians because we are afraid His power won't work outside our local church building.

Satan also holds us back because we don't want to be "different." But God wants us to be different! He wants us to know we're backed by heaven, not by this world's system. When we go out into the world, we're not taking a chance. If we lay hands on our unsaved loved ones who are sick, they will recover by the healing power of God we have released in our faith-filled words. If we are laid off from that secular job, our income won't change because God has already provided something better. We are kingdom ambassadors sent to the world to conduct government business in Jesus' name. The devil is so happy when believers don't come out of the four walls of the church. He revels in the fact that most of us don't yet know who we are—that we are royalty and more than conquerors in the eyes of God. He gets excited when we see the world as the enemy instead of God's harvest of souls. But the devil is losing this battle because believers are awakening to the gospel of the kingdom and beginning to take it by force.

THE VIOLENT TAKE IT BY FORCE

God wants us to remember that no matter who in the world we don't like, He loves them and wants them saved. He wants us to see that the church building is not a place to hide. It's a place to be filled up with His Word and power to go out there

73

and do damage to the kingdom of darkness. He wants us to know that when we're out in the harvest, everything we need has been provided.

Jesus said that the violent take the kingdom by force (Matt. 11:12). Ironically, the toughest guy in the world will often become "too nice" after he becomes born again. When he sees his neighbor's teenager getting in trouble, he'll say, "Oh, I don't want to say anything that'll offend anybody." Instead, he ought to look that rebellious kid in the eye and say, "You're going to be saved." We need to stop letting people intimidate us! We are well able to take the kingdom of God and bring it to earth in full demonstration.

Paul said, "I'm a fool for Christ" (1 Cor. 4:10). We've been trying to compromise and conform to the world, but we don't have to do that. God has placed something in us that can't be found in the whole world. We were born in this hour because we are exactly who He wants to demonstrate His kingdom to now, in our world.

God doesn't look at our flesh because flesh makes mistakes. He doesn't look at our mind because our mind can't figure it out. He just looks to Jesus because He's the author and finisher of our faith, and He's going to take us where we're supposed to go.

We are the people God needs for this hour, but if we're not wise about the devices of the enemy, condemnation will block us out of kingdom provisions. When people are religious, trying to prove themselves worthy to God (which no one but Jesus can), they get condemned and the enemy steals everything they have. The kingdom of God isn't about religious rituals and works and proving ourselves worthy to God. It's about accepting that we can never be worthy and receiving Jesus' righteousness. If we're seeking first the kingdom of God *and His righteousness,* then we are entitled to the kingdom provisions (Matt. 6:33) because His righteousness deserves it.

You need to get violent and start speaking the truth of the kingdom. For example, if you don't have enough money to pay all the bills, take your pocketbook out, put it on the table, and say, "You're filled up. God supplies all my needs according to His riches in glory." That's God talk. That's taking the kingdom by force. We have to get out of our mind and speak to the problem according to God's Word.

We must remember that the kingdom of God is in us, and it is a spiritual kingdom. We were meant to receive provision for our lives from our spirits. When God loaded the kingdom in us, He designed it to supply our every need. Any one of us could be injured and alone up on Mount Vesuvius, no doctor present, and the kingdom in us would supply our healing. That's the power of the kingdom in us.

I believe we've been too conservative about taking the kingdom in the past, but we're able now. Let's go at once and possess it! This is our time. God chose us for this hour. We must take the kingdom by force and demonstrate the lordship of Jesus to this corrupt world.

CHAPTER 6

DEMONSTRATING THE KINGDOM IN A CORRUPT WORLD

The present world's system is failing. The Bible says that the enemy is so deceptive that, if it were possible, he would deceive the very elect (Matt. 24:24). However, he will not deceive those who have the kingdom inside and who learn to operate in it. As God's people, we must rise above the failing world's system and demonstrate the kingdom to the people of the earth.

The devil wants people to believe that the world's system is a good one. He deceives people, and then the deceived people begin to deceive others. For example, think about the companies and individuals who have gone from great wealth to bankruptcy or jail because they have been deceived and have tried to deceive others. They were working a failing system, which, by the way, is Satan's most deceptive and successful theft. Jesus teaches in Matthew 12:33 that we can't get good fruit out of a bad tree; if the tree is corrupt, the fruit will be corrupt.

For a time, it may seem that the world's system works. However, Proverbs 14:12 says, "There is a way which seemeth right unto a man, but the end thereof are the ways of death." The world is corrupt because its way of doing things is not based on God's kingdom. It's still based on Satan's system, which fallen human beings operate. Satan knows people on the earth caught in his system have to obey or be supplied from another kingdom.

God may place some of His own people in companies in which the leaders are advancing by deception, but He places them there with the understanding that they don't have to live by that system. One of my definitions of the kingdom of God is being ruled by the Word of God in our heart rather than controlled by some external system or source.

James 1:13-15 says,

> Let no man say when he is tempted, I am tempted of God: for God cannot be tempted with evil, neither tempteth he any man: but every man is tempted, when he is drawn away of his own lust, and enticed. Then when lust hath conceived, it bringeth forth sin: and sin, when it is finished, bringeth forth death.

Anything that is built and based on sin will eventually die. The world's social system is deteriorating. Crime is not only increasing, but the wickedness of crimes has become more diverse. Today we have everything from terrorists and gangs in our cities to child pornographers on the Internet to identity theft and all kinds of "white collar" crime. The Bible says that perilous times will come in the last days. However, if we come out of the world's system and enter God's system, we will be satisfied and protected, and we will bring light into the darkness of our time.

DELIVERANCE FROM SIN, SICKNESS, AND OPPRESSION

Only those who separate themselves from this world's system will be able to enter God's system. First Corinthians 6:9-11 (AMP) says,

> *Do you not know that the unrighteous and the wrong-doers will not inherit or have any share in the kingdom of God? Do not be deceived (misled): neither the impure and immoral, nor idolaters, nor adulterers, nor those who participate in homosexuality, nor cheats (swindlers and thieves), nor greedy graspers, nor drunkards, nor foulmouthed revilers and slanderers, nor extortioners and robbers will inherit or have any share in the kingdom of God.*
>
> *And such some of you were [once]. But you were washed clean (purified by a complete atonement for sin and made free from the guilt of sin), and you were consecrated (set apart, hallowed), and you were justified [pronounced righteous, by trusting] in the name of the Lord Jesus Christ and in the [Holy] Spirit of our God.*

Once a person has been born again, they have been delivered from the power of darkness by the power of God.

Sometimes people in the world's system who are in bondage to habitual sin will say, "Well, I can't help this." However, God has a way for us to escape every sin. Satan has deceived the people in this world. They live in an entirely corrupt system. But when they seek the kingdom of God, God will not leave them the way they are.

First John 3:8 AMP says,

> *[But] he who commits sin [who practices evildoing] is of the devil [takes his character from the evil one], for the devil has sinned (violated the divine law) from the beginning. The reason the Son of God was made manifest (visible) was to undo (destroy, loosen, and dissolve) the works the devil [has done].*

God sent His Son, Jesus, to turn around, reverse, and undo everything the devil has done. Whatever habitual sin someone may feel stuck in, no matter how bad and how deep it is inside of them, Jesus has set them free.

Most people don't know the power of the kingdom of God. Psalm 103:19 says, "The Lord hath prepared his throne in the heavens; and his kingdom ruleth over all." Furthermore, 1 Corinthians 4:20 says, "For the kingdom of God is not in word, but in power." The power of God's kingdom is greater than the power of any other kingdom, and it is available to restore every unbeliever (or believer) who is bound by sin in this world. It comes with enough power to reverse any curse, to restore all that sin destroyed.

Matthew 24:14 says,

And this gospel of the kingdom shall be preached in all the world for a witness unto all nations; and then shall the end come.

The end will come because the world will see God's power on the earth through His church. This is what Jesus came to the earth and sent us into the world to do: to clean up everything the devil messed up; to restore the whole earth from everything the devil has done to it. It makes no difference how long anyone has struggled with sin, the power of the kingdom has broken the chains and set them free.

Mark 5 describes a man whose life was overtaken by demon spirits. When Jesus came to the coast where the man endured a terrible existence, He cast out every one of those spirits, and the man was completely restored.

If demon spirits are causing a person to do something that no mere human solution can fix, the power of the Lord Jesus Christ is available to fix it. He left the power of His kingdom here with the church to fix anything that is broken.

Someone might say, "Well, I was born like this, so nothing can change me." Acts 3 tells the story of a man who was born disabled. Into his adulthood he still had never walked. Daily he was placed at the temple gate called Beautiful. When Peter and John passed by, the man looked to them and expected alms. However, Peter said, "Silver and gold have I none; but such as I have give I thee: In the name of Jesus Christ of Nazareth rise up and walk" (v. 6). At that moment, everything in that man's body straightened out, and he was made whole.

Every sickness, every disease, every infirmity, every demon possession among the people—Jesus healed them all (Matt. 12:15). And the Scripture says, "Jesus Christ is the same yesterday, today, and forever" (Heb. 13:8). If we're dealing with any sin, sickness, or oppression, all we need to do is come to God, seek the kingdom of God, ask for deliverance, and by faith receive His power to deliver us all.

THE ECONOMY-LIFESTYLE LINK

It is this power of God's kingdom that we have to share with our neighbors, coworkers, and friends. The world's system is collapsing, and they need the kingdom so that they too can escape what is coming to the earth.

Psalm 107:33-34 says,

> *He turneth rivers into a wilderness, and the watersprings into dry ground; a fruitful land into barrenness, for the wickedness of them that dwell therein.*

Galatians 6:7-8 says,

> *Be not deceived; God is not mocked: for whatsoever a man soweth, that shall he also reap. For he that soweth to his flesh shall of the flesh reap corruption; but he that soweth to the Spirit shall of the Spirit reap life everlasting.*

The Amplified Bible says, "For he who sows to his own flesh (lower nature, sensuality) will from the flesh reap decay and ruin and destruction." The economy and fruitfulness of the land are linked to the lifestyles of the people living in it. The signs are everywhere. Something is coming, and the world's system is about to collapse. Why? It's the judgment or harvest from the seeds of fleshly works. However, when the world's system fails, God's kingdom will prevail.

God needs us to walk in the reality of His kingdom. It is a spiritual reality that we can only see and demonstrate if our eyes are single, totally devoted to Him.

> *The light of the body is the eye: if therefore thine eye be single, thy whole body shall be full of light.*
>
> MATTHEW 6:22

Jesus came demonstrating the kingdom of God. He healed the sick, raised the dead, cleansed the lepers, and gave sight to the blind. He fed five thousand with two fish and five loaves of bread. He forgave a woman who had been caught in the sin of adultery. These were all demonstrations of the kingdom of God at work, and these are the demonstrations that He will continue to show the world through us.

In the midst of an economic collapse, God's people will draw from heavenly provisions, being supplied by another kingdom, to not only sustain themselves and their families but also to reach out to the people of the world and draw them into the kingdom. How will they do that? Matthew 6:33 says, "Seek ye first the kingdom of God, and his righteousness; and all these things shall be added unto you." They will always be focused on Jesus and His kingdom.

Because of what Jesus did for us, we should be reigning in life. Romans 5:17 says,

> *For if by one man's offence death reigned by one; much more they which receive abundance of grace and of the gift of righteousness shall reign in life by one, Jesus Christ.*

The Amplified Bible says we "reign as kings." Not only should we reign when we get to heaven and the millennial reign in Christ, but we should reign in this life for the world to see. To do that, we need a revelation of our righteousness in Christ Jesus and an abundance of His grace.

THE KINGDOM BASED ON GRACE

If the kingdom were conditional on our own faithfulness, ability, or goodness, none of us could reign in this life and inherit the kingdom of God. But, thank God, it is not conditional on what we can do; it is conditional on what He already did. Jesus makes this clear while talking about John the Baptist in Matthew 11:11.

> *Verily I say unto you, Among them that are born of women there hath not risen a greater than John the Baptist: notwithstanding he that is least in the kingdom of heaven is greater than he.*

John the Baptist was a holy man, an esteemed example of a life devoted to God. However, Jesus said he who is least in the kingdom is greater than John the Baptist. Stumbling, bumbling new Christians are greater than John the Baptist because they are partakers of God's grace and have been justified by faith. They are under no condemnation, and God has removed all their sins as far as the east is from the west. God will remember their sins no more (Ps. 103:12; Jer. 31:34).

Some people say that we're going to be without a spot or wrinkle when Jesus comes back. However, with His righteousness, we're without spot or wrinkle right now. It's no longer our works that qualify us. We are qualified by Jesus' works. His works are ours by faith.

We're supposed to seek first the kingdom of God and His righteousness because through His righteousness we operate in the kingdom of God. Because of Jesus' work, we are no longer under the Law of Moses. We are saved by grace and now operate in the kingdom by grace (Eph. 2:8.)

The reason some of God's people don't live in the kingdom reality is that they deal with condemnation and a sense of unrighteousness. It's true that under the Old Covenant there was no final redemption for sin, but Jesus made the way for us to receive His righteousness and freed us from condemnation. He opened the eternal door to a new and better covenant. Jeremiah 31:31-34 says,

> *Behold, the days come, saith the Lord, that I will make a new covenant with the house of Israel, and with the house of Judah: not according to the covenant that I made with their fathers in the day that I took them by the hand to bring them out of the land of Egypt; which my covenant they brake, although I was an husband unto them, saith the Lord: but this shall be the covenant that I will make with the house of Israel; after those days, saith the Lord, I will put my law in their*

inward parts, and write it in their hearts; and will be their God, and they shall be my people. And they shall teach no more every man his neighbour, and every man his brother, saying, Know the Lord: for they shall all know me, from the least of them unto the greatest of them, saith the Lord: for I will forgive their iniquity, and I will remember their sin no more.

Jesus came with grace and truth, and He came to do away with the law. Now God has written the law in our hearts. He guides us by the Holy Spirit. Not only that, but once we come to the Father through Jesus, God has no record of our sins and failures. The only thing on record now is the righteous deeds we do by walking according to the Spirit and not the flesh. That is a wonderful thing! That is freedom!

This is the Good News we need to share with the world, because when they don't know this, the enemy burdens them with condemnation for sin. This is one of his methods of trying to control the masses. But when they hear about the grace that is extended to them in Jesus Christ, Satan's deceptions and lies are exposed and they are set free.

WHEN WORLDLY GOVERNMENT OPPOSES GOD'S GOVERNMENT

Second Kings 21:1-2 says,

Manasseh was twelve years old when he began to reign, and reigned fifty and five years in Jerusalem.... And he did that which was evil in the sight of the Lord, after the abominations of the heathen, whom the Lord cast out before the children of

Israel. Among his other abominable offenses, King Manasseh sacrificed his sons in the Valley of Hinom where the people offered their children up to Molech.

Verses 11-12 say,

> *Because Manasseh king of Judah hath done these abom-*
> *inations, and hath done wickedly above all that the*
> *Amorites did, which were before him, and hath made*
> *Judah also to sin with his idols: therefore thus saith the*
> *Lord God of Israel, Behold, I am bringing such evil*
> *upon Jerusalem and Judah, that whosoever heareth of*
> *it, both his ears shall tingle.*

Verse 16 says,

> *Moreover Manasseh shed innocent blood very much, till*
> *he had filled Jerusalem from one end to another; beside*
> *his sin wherewith he made Judah to sin, in doing that*
> *which was evil in the sight of the Lord.*

Notice that Manasseh "made Judah to sin." The lesson in his story is that as the leaders go, so go the people. King Manasseh shed innocent blood, sacrificing sons to his god, and this deed was tantamount to today's abortion and genocide.

In Manasseh's day and in our day, the will of God has always been that His people be under His government and not the government of this world's system. He never intended that humans should make laws that are contrary to God's laws.

In our nation, the founders used the Bible as a source for lawmaking, but today we frequently see an interpretation of the law that is contrary to the original intent or the Word of God. What the saints have to do is come back to the Bible. We have to let the Word of God be our judge. If anyone—including our earthly leaders—strays away from the Word of God, we have to stay with the Word. If our aim is to be socially acceptable or intellectually approved by man, we might please men but definitely miss the kingdom of God.

In Chapter 3 of this book, we saw how Daniel was an exemplary model of one who honored God's law over human law. The Bible says he had an excellent spirit, and because he had such gifts and talents God raised him up as a leader in the Medo-Persian kingdom. However, because he was doing so well, his colleagues became jealous and wanted to do away with him. As hard as they tried, though, they couldn't find fault with him.

> *Then said these men, We shall not find any occasion against this Daniel, except we find it against him concerning the law of his God. Then these presidents and princes assembled together to the king, and said thus unto him, King Darius, live for ever. All the presidents of the kingdom, the governors, and the princes, the counsellors, and the captains, have consulted together to establish a royal statute, and to make a firm decree, that whosoever shall ask a petition of any God or man for thirty days, save of thee, O king, he shall be cast into the den of lions. Now, O king, establish the decree, and sign the writing, that it be not changed, according to the law of the Medes and Persians, which altereth not.*
>
> DANIEL 6:5-7

Remember: The Medo-Persian kingdom was operated by a rule of law, which meant the laws could not be changed.

Verses 9-10 continue:

> *Wherefore king Darius signed the writing and the decree. Now when Daniel knew that the writing was signed, he went into his house; and his windows being open in his chamber toward Jerusalem, he kneeled upon his knees three times a day, and prayed, and gave thanks before his God, as he did aforetime.*

Daniel knew well that the law had been signed and could not be reversed, but he didn't let the law change him because he knew whom he served. He knew that because he served God and was under His kingdom and government, he had God's protection. He was thrown into the lions' den but lived to tell about it.

> *Then said Daniel unto the king, O king, live for ever. My God hath sent his angel, and hath shut the lions' mouths, that they have not hurt me: forasmuch as before him innocency was found in me; and also before thee, O king, have I done no hurt.*
>
> *Then was the king exceedingly glad for him, and commanded that they should take Daniel up out of the den. So Daniel was taken up out of the den, and no manner of hurt was found upon him, because he believed in his God.*
>
> DANIEL 6:21-23

So many people today are trying to straddle the fence between living by God's Word and living according to the laws of their land, but it doesn't work like that. No man can serve two masters. Jesus said, "If therefore thine eye be single, thy whole body shall be full of light" (Matt. 6:22). If we serve God with all our heart, our whole body will be full of light.

God looks at the heart. If we're not intending to follow Him, we will receive neither His revelation nor His kingdom. On the other hand, if we are like Daniel, focusing on God's kingdom and His righteousness in the midst of this corrupt world, we will inherit the kingdom, and we will live to tell about it.

CHAPTER 7

OPERATING IN
THE KINGDOM

We have the kingdom, we are ambassadors and citizens of another government, meaning that heaven is our country, but now we need to learn how to operate in the kingdom. There are laws and a constitution for operating in the kingdom of God, just as there are laws for operating in the world's governments. When we understand the laws of God's system, we can access our inheritance and live the abundant life that Jesus provides for His own (John 10:10.)

In Luke 16, Jesus tells the story of a man who worked for a rich man and wasted his goods. The rich man called him in and said, "Give an account of your stewardship, for you can no longer be steward" (v. 2). In other words, he was going to fire him. To save his position, the steward ran out and started making deals with the rich man's debtors. To someone who owed his master a hundred measures of oil, the steward said, "Take thy bill, and sit down quickly, and write fifty" (v. 6). He offered similar deals with every one of his lord's debtors. Each debtor gladly gave him what he asked. When his boss saw what he had done, he "commended the unjust steward, because he had done wisely" (v. 8).

After telling this story, Jesus said, "The children of this world are in their generation wiser than the children of light" (v. 8). Jesus was saying, in essence, "This dishonest man worked a dishonest system and increased. The children of light are in an honest system—the kingdom of God. Why don't they work the system I have given them so that they can increase?"

The wicked increase because they work the wicked system. God's people have a better system, and they need to work that system because the kingdom of God rules over all other systems. Up to this time it seems that what Jesus said is true. The people of the world are much wiser in their use of the world's system than the children of God are in using the system of the kingdom of God.

The children of light just let the kingdom of God sit inside of them and do nothing. Meanwhile, the children of darkness have been working the kingdom of this world. They're busy cheating on income tax, robbing pensions, defrauding and underpaying, telling people lies, or making inferior products. I'm not saying all people in the world do that, but some folks do. They're working a wicked system to get ahead, and that's what Satan wants. He wants to keep the resources of the world under the control of the kingdom of darkness.

We need to say, "Wait a minute! I have the kingdom of God in me, and this kingdom can produce everything needed in abundance! We need to work the system of the kingdom of God and set a new standard for the world as His ambassadors.

For example, the kingdom of God gives a hundredfold return on seed planted. A hundredfold return will affect people for miles around. A hundredfold in our marriages will affect every relative we have. A hundredfold of joy will affect everybody around us. A hundredfold in our finances will enable us to take care of everybody we meet who has a need.

The trouble is that we're still trying to work a little of the world's system and a little of God's system. It's time to come out of the world's system and live according to the kingdom inside of us. For those who obey Him, the King gives power and ability without measure.

THE HEART'S TREASURE

The kingdom is in us. Jesus talked about having this system inside when He said,

> *Either make the tree good, and his fruit good; or else make the tree corrupt, and his fruit corrupt: for the tree is known by his fruit. O generation of vipers, how can ye, being evil, speak good things? for out of the abundance of the heart the mouth speaketh. A good man out of the good treasure of the heart bringeth forth good things: and an evil man out of the evil treasure bringeth forth evil things.*
> MATTHEW 12:33-35

What comes forth in our lives comes from our hearts. This is why God desires to change the hearts of unbelievers by the new birth and then the renewing of their minds by His Word. The treasure in our hearts is Jesus, the Living Word.

Jesus referred to the good or evil "treasure" of a person's heart. We could call that treasure a deposit and read the verse this way: "A good person out of the good deposit of the heart brings forth good things, and an evil person out of the evil deposit of the heart brings forth evil things."

What we deposit in our hearts is what our lives will produce. A good deposit will yield good things in our lives, and an evil deposit will yield evil things. These "evil things" are all the things that oppose our health, wealth, and human existence. They are things that are not from Him but from the devil (John 10:10). These "good things" are the fruit and power of the Holy Spirit, which come from consistently sowing God's Word in our hearts.

Whatever is being produced in our lives is coming from our heart. Our provision is not from "The Man" and not from a paycheck. It's from the treasure of the Word of God in our hearts because that's how God made His system to work.

LETTING GO OF A PAYCHECK MENTALITY

Most of us have been programmed with a paycheck mentality, but that is not the way God's system works. When Israel was in Egypt, they worked as slaves. Then when God delivered them and they came into the wilderness, He provided for them. They learned that they didn't necessarily need a job.

I'm not suggesting that anyone should just quit their job. However, we need to recognize that our source and supply are not a job. God gave Adam work, not a job. Work and a job are two different things. A job is for making money, but work is for manifesting our potential, and for that we end up getting paid. Many people go to their jobs on Monday mornings looking miserable because they're on their way to a job they can't stand. Some people are doing a job that is not their work. It is not what God called them to do, so it is not drawing out the gift that God has placed inside of them. Therefore, it provides them no fulfillment.

The purpose for work is to manifest our potential so that we can serve others and serve God better. That is how we will find fulfillment in what we do.

People have attached their worth to their job, and they've attached their paycheck to what they can have. Both of these assumptions are false. One way Satan keeps people bound is by convincing them that their paycheck is all there is, and their job is all they are.

After their exodus from Egypt, God wanted to show His people that they didn't even need a paycheck. They didn't need any human providing their material needs (Ex. 16). He wanted them to know, and He wants us to know, that He can provide for His people without a paycheck. It's not done in the natural; it's done by the spirit.

God also wants us to do the work He has called us to do. He wants us to know that in Him we have genius in us. Satan's goal is to divert us from our gift and calling and have us just doing a job (unless it's used for his benefit), but God wants to get us back into the work He has for us. And He wants to show us that He can provide more than enough for us even if the work we are doing shuts down.

In the kingdom, God's assignment could send us to work temporarily at McDonald's. It wouldn't be a job; it would be our work. He could send us there because in six months someone would come in hungry for more than a burger. They'd come in looking for eternal hope, and we'd be there to offer them the kingdom. We could work at McDonald's and still have a corporate jet. Why? Because increase in the kingdom doesn't come by what you sell, but what you sow. The kingdom is the only place we could do that because it isn't based on a paycheck. It's based on God's Word and what we believe.

BLESSINGS FROM THE INSIDE OUT

God's system is one of supernatural deposit and return: A good man out of the deposit of his heart brings forth good things. Good things come from the deposit of the Word of God in our hearts. They don't come from the world. The enemy tricks us into thinking that our blessings, healing, and every good provision come from the outside in. However, the truth is that they come from the inside out. In fact, our entire lives are lived from the inside out. Our thoughts and beliefs concerning God's Word manifest in our deeds, and thus our lives reflect the Word of God that is inside us.

Matthew 12:34-35 says,

> *For out of the abundance of the heart the mouth speaketh. A good man out of the good treasure of the heart bringeth forth good things.*

When Jesus told His disciples to feed the five thousand (Matt. 15), they were probably thinking, "Now wait a minute, Boss. You know we just left our jobs about eight months ago."

However, God is in the business of placing a demand on us beyond our natural resources and ability. He does it on purpose because He wants to manifest who He really is and who we really are. We are spirit, in a flesh body, and our supply comes not from a job but from the Word we know and believe within.

WORKING THE SYSTEM

Jesus said, "Seek ye first the kingdom of God, and his righteousness; and all these *things* shall be added unto you" (Matt. 6:33, emphasis added). He also said, "Your Father knoweth what things ye have need of, before ye ask him" (Matt. 6:8).

When I was a full-time Bible school student in Tulsa, my wife and I began to work the system of God's kingdom by looking to access employment for my wife. People were being laid off by the hundreds, but we had the kingdom of God, which is designed to produce a harvest independent of what's going on around us.

First, my wife and I started pursuing her new employment with the Word. Every pursuit in God's system starts with the Word because it is the seed that produces what we need. My wife and I wrote scriptures on index cards and placed them around the house to remind us of God's promises. For example, when we opened the refrigerator, we saw the card that said, "We are redeemed from the curse" (Gal. 3:13). We kept the Word before us because Proverbs 4:20-22 says we are to keep it in our eyes, our ears, and our heart.

When a friend came to visit and asked, "Veronica, do you have the job yet?" she said, "Yup, sure do." She didn't have it in the natural, but in the spirit she had already received it by faith. That's the way the Spirit of God produces.

Then my friend asked, "Where is it?" and she said, "I don't know where it is, but I have it." She was operating in the kingdom of God, trusting the Word of the King completely to supply the work she needed. She took her eyes off the world and focused them on God and His ability to provide for her.

For us to operate in the kingdom of God, we have to trust Him alone. We can't serve two masters. We have to choose whom we will serve and trust. Jesus told the rich young ruler that if he would sell everything, give it to the poor, and follow Him, he'd have treasure in heaven. Then He said, "Take up the cross, and follow me" (Mark 10:21). Jesus wasn't telling the rich young ruler to go broke. He was telling him that he could make a deposit of faith in Him and receive everything he would ever need from His kingdom.

When we deposit our treasure in heaven by having faith in His Word, God multiplies it and gives us back more than we can contain. When we need it, all we have to do is call for it. We can let heaven be our reservoir, our bank, and our depository, because He said, "Where your treasure is, there will your heart be also" (Luke 12:34). We're not to place our trust in the stock market; we're to place our trust in God.

Regardless of what happens to the world's system, we'll always have more than enough when we have laid up our treasure in heaven. We can call for it when we need it and where we need it because the wealth of God is infinitely portable. When Peter told Jesus that they needed tax money, Jesus didn't say, "Peter, go get a second job. Work the night shift." No, He said, "Go to the river, and throw in a hook. The first fish you pull up will have the money in its mouth. Use it to pay our taxes"

(Matt. 17:27). Jesus had laid up His treasure in heaven, and that treasure was made available on earth when He needed it.

When we give an offering, we lay up treasure in heaven. God records that offering in the heavens, adds a hundredfold to it, and makes it available for us when we need it.

There is more than enough in God's kingdom. God knew that we were going to be in the earth. He knew there would be times when we would need something beyond our natural resources, so He placed within us a system that would provide more than enough.

My wife could have said, "Well, I guess there aren't any jobs," but she didn't. She worked the system. God prompted her to write her job of choice on an index card, so she wrote, "I want a job in computers. I want a nice office ten minutes from the house. I want [this salary], and I want a car with it."

While no one was hiring in town, and many were being laid off, my wife got a call for an interview. God's system doesn't care what everybody else has or is doing. The system will work for us.

However, God will allow what we'll allow. The Bible says He knows what we have need of even before we ask Him. Nevertheless, we have to ask Him (Matt. 6:32,33). It just doesn't automatically happen. We've got to work the system. We have to ask according to His Word.

When my wife went to check out that job, she learned how well God's system works. The job was in computers, in a nice office about ten minutes from the house, paid five thousand dollars more than she had written on the card at home, and came with a new Buick that she got to pick out for herself!

You may not need a job, but you may need something else. No matter what you need, God has already provided it. He is Jehovah Jireh, your provider. He sees and has already provided everything you need in abundance.

REWARDS IN HEAVEN

Once we understand how to work God's system for everything we need, we will begin to say and do things that unbelievers and believers who still have no revelation of the kingdom of God will not understand. Some will persecute us for having faith in God and His Word instead of our paycheck, for finding our value in Him instead of the work He's called us to do. Some people will try to hold us back. They'll persecute us by talking badly about our church and the steps we're taking to better our lives.

Matthew 5:11-12 says we are to rejoice when we're persecuted because when we do, rewards are sent up to heaven. When we're persecuted, we're not supposed to say, "You know what she said about me? I can't stand her anyway." Instead, we're supposed to say, "Praise God! You are taking care of me." It's part of working the system.

You have to rejoice and forgive them, but you also have to say, "Persecution can't hold me back." Maybe you've been letting blessings pass you by for years because persecution distracts you from pursuing God's best for you. This time when persecution comes, start jumping up and down, saying, "This is my hour! This is the time of my rejoicing for all the rewards I'm getting in heaven because I believed God and His Word inside me!"

CALLED AWAY FROM THE WORLD'S PROVISION

In Matthew 19:27, Peter said to Jesus, "Behold, we have forsaken all, and followed thee; what shall we have therefore?" Jesus said, "And every one that hath forsaken houses, or brethren, or sisters, or father, or mother, or wife, or children, or lands, for my name's sake, shall receive an hundredfold, and shall inherit everlasting life" (v. 29).

When God was calling me to go into ministry full time, at first I just couldn't go. I was bound to the world's system. I was deep in debt. I had religion and Bible verses, but I didn't have revelation. Finally, I listened and meditated and received the revelation that I could no longer serve God and money. I began to see myself as God saw me.

When I told my boss I was leaving, he sat back in his chair and squinted his eyes. He said, "Take two weeks off." He thought I'd been working too hard.

So I took two weeks off and got into the Word of God. As soon as I got back, my boss called me in to his office to find out how I was doing. He thought I had recovered. He said, "How do you feel about the job now?"

I said, "John, not only am I leaving, but I'm leaving now."

What had happened during my two weeks in God's Word was that I converted my job to a heavenly deposit. In obedience to God's calling, I planted the seed of the Word in my heart and made my deposit in the kingdom of God. In other words, I worked the system.

Satan's system had been working me, but the kingdom of God rules over all. When I took the leap of faith into the kingdom of God and went into full-time ministry, one of the rewards I saw in this life was that God brought me totally out of debt. I saw right away that God's provision through faith in His Word was much better than the world's provision through faith in a paycheck!

OPERATING IN THE SPIRIT

To live in the kingdom and work God's system, we have to operate from the spirit. Why? Because His system operates by faith. God didn't make us to live naturally. The natural realm only provides experiences, not life. True living comes by faith in God.

We can't live by faith in the natural. Faith is a spiritual reality only God can provide (Eph. 2:8). When we are operating by faith in God, we can withdraw what we need from our heavenly account. Our heavenly account is above the world's system, so Satan can't touch it. Inflation and depression can't touch it. If we go to another continent we can withdraw it right there because we are carrying the treasure of God's exceeding great and precious promises in our heart.

What we need to always remember is that this is not natural wisdom. Flesh and blood cannot inherit the kingdom of God. We cannot forget that. The kingdom of God is not for flesh but for spirit. What comes out of our lives comes from our spirits, or our hearts.

In the kingdom of God, the condition of our hearts determines the condition of our lives. A good tree can't bring forth bad fruit. What's in our lives in the unseen realm will manifest in the seen realm. If we're broke on the outside, it's because we're broke inside. We have an image of ourselves as broke. At some time the world's system, our family, or somebody put an image inside of us that's not from God. That's why we have struggled every step of the way. However, as we meditate on God's Word, we will tear down the distorted image the devil placed in our hearts and build the image of our redemption in Christ.

We cannot receive our inheritance from the kingdom of God without walking in the spirit, and we cannot walk in the spirit without walking in God's Word. We are going to work God's kingdom system by reading and speaking and meditating on the Word. We are going to plant Word seeds, for Jesus said, "The sower soweth the word" (Mark 4:14), and we will harvest the good fruit of God's kingdom.

Psalm 115:14 says, "The Lord shall increase you more and more, you and your children." We and our families will experience the promises of the kingdom everywhere we go when we walk according to the Spirit and not our flesh, when we continually sow His Word in our hearts and live from our heavenly bank account instead of the world's system and way of thinking.

THE DEVIL CAN'T TOUCH OUR HEAVENLY ACCOUNT

In Daniel 10, we read about an angel who said,

> *O Daniel, a man greatly beloved, understand the words that I speak unto thee, and stand upright: for unto thee am I now sent....*
>
> *Fear not, Daniel: for from the first day that thou didst set thine heart to understand, and to chasten thyself*

before thy God, thy words were heard, and I am come for thy words. But the prince of the kingdom of Persia withstood me one and twenty days: but, lo, Michael, one of the chief princes, came to help me; and I remained there with the kings of Persia.

DANIEL 10:11-13

God has provided everything we need. He has answered our prayers. Now we've got to keep praising Him for that, because a war is being waged in the heavenlies.

The world's system is crumbling under the deceptive control of demonic spirits. Its government is corrupt and led by a thief. This is why God says to not store up our treasure in this world's system, because the thief may break through and get it (Matt. 6:20). What we have to do, instead, is to deposit our treasure on a higher plane, in heaven.

This is what Jesus did, and no thief could touch His treasury. John 12:1-2 says,

Then Jesus six days before the passover came to Bethany, where Lazarus was, which had been dead, whom he raised from the dead. There they made him a supper; and Martha served: but Lazarus was one of them that sat at the table with him.

Lazarus had been sick and had even died, but God had raised him. Now he was sitting in the room with Jesus and his sisters, Mary and Martha, getting ready to eat the Passover supper.

Then took Mary a pound of ointment of spikenard, very costly, and anointed the feet of Jesus, and wiped his feet

with her hair: and the house was filled with the odour
of the ointment.

Then saith one of his disciples, Judas Iscariot, Simon's
son, which should betray him, Why was not this oint-
ment sold for three hundred pence, and given to the
poor?

JOHN 12:3-5

God is not financing poverty. He is out to destroy it. He wants us to give to poor people, but not to foster their dependence on us. We have to always point them to the true Provider. We have to get them off the world's system and point them to God's system and kingdom, a place where they can be blessed and be a blessing to others.

Jesus gave to the poor, but He didn't encourage them to live off welfare generation after generation. In verse 6, we find the cause for Judas's accusation.

This he said, not that he cared for the poor; but because
he was a thief, and had the bag, and bare what was put
therein.

Judas was a thief, and as Jesus' treasurer he was stealing Jesus' ministry money. Some folks think that Jesus was broke, but how many broke people have you seen who have a treasurer? Judas was stealing, but as quickly as he could steal it, more came in. You can't steal from a man and have no one notice unless that man has a lot of money! You also cannot empty the bank account of someone who has a revelation of their kingdom identity.

We may have deposits in heaven right now that we need to withdraw. The devil can't touch our account any more than he could touch Jesus' account. God has it, and it's for us. God had us sow His Word in our hearts and live according to His Word, and now He wants us to reap the good harvest of the good seed we have sown.

The gospel of Jesus Christ brought us salvation, and the gospel of the kingdom will teach us how to live now that we have been saved. As we learn the principles of God's kingdom and apply them to our lives, we will experience a whole new life of victory. We will make our deposits in heaven, and we will receive an abundant return from God when we need it. We will be free from the corruption of the world's system, and we will walk in the liberty of God's kingdom and made my deposit in the kingdom of God. In other words, I worked the system.

Satan's system had been working me, but the kingdom of God rules over all. When I took the leap of faith into the kingdom of God and went into full-time ministry, one of the rewards I saw in this life was that God brought me totally out of debt. I saw right away that God's provision through faith in His Word was much better than the world's provision through faith in a paycheck!

CHAPTER 8

THE PRINCIPLES OF GOD'S KINGDOM

God's kingdom is not of this world, but it works in this earth because He put it inside of us. However, we have to work the principles of the kingdom in order to receive its benefits. We find the principles of the kingdom of God in the Bible. Therefore, we will need to know the truth of God's Word to understand how His kingdom works.

God has designed His kingdom to function in a certain way. In order to separate ourselves from the world's system and operate in God's system, we need to seek and live by the truth of the Word. The truth will make us free from the entanglements of the world's system. Jesus said,

> *If ye continue in my word, then are ye my disciples indeed; and ye shall know the truth, and the truth shall make you free.*
>
> JOHN 8:31-32

Without the truth, we can't break free from the world's system. And as we have discussed, Satan holds people in bondage through the world's system. If they do not hear or see the truth of God's Word, they don't know there is any other way to live. Remember, as kingdom citizens we are in the world but not of the world. The church is not to withdraw in seclusion for fear of being contaminated, for we are the light of the world.

THE HAND OF THE WICKED

In Psalm 82:3-5 the psalmist intercedes for those locked in Satan's bonds.

> *Defend the poor and fatherless: do justice to the afflicted and needy. Deliver the poor and needy: rid them out of the hand of the wicked. They know not, neither will they understand; they walk on in darkness: all the foundations of the earth are out of course.*

This whole world's system is established on a foundation that God didn't build. Satan can't create anything, and he can't think of anything new, so he took God's pattern and perverted it. The reason he is able to manipulate people is that they have no relationship with God or revelation of His kingdom. He can thus work through blinded people to continue to build his dark kingdom.

Satan, in an effort to overtake God's kingdom, even tried to blind its King with the temptation of the world's provision.

> *And the devil, taking him up into an high mountain, shewed unto him all the kingdoms of the world in a*

> *moment of time. And the devil said unto him, All this*
> *power will I give thee, and the glory of them: for that is*
> *delivered unto me; and to whomsoever I will I give it.*
> *If thou therefore wilt worship me, all shall be thine.*
>
> LUKE 4:5-7

If Satan had been successful in getting Jesus to worship him, his kingdom of darkness and its evil system would have overtaken all the people of the earth. However, Jesus resisted him with the truth of the Word of God (vv. 4,8,12) and ultimately offered the keys of the kingdom to all who would receive Him. Now that He has given us the keys of His kingdom (Matt. 16:19), we can operate in it and successfully resist the devil with the truth of God's Word.

Satan is behind a system that is controlling the economics of this world, man-made religions, and political processes. But when we have the kingdom inside, we can rule over everything Satan has established.

Satan also doesn't want anyone to know that he is behind the world's system. He's like the guy who throws the rock and hides his hand. Or he tells people who get hurt that God hurt them. The devil's the one who hurts people, but he points the finger at God to keep them from trusting Him and leaving the kingdom of darkness for the kingdom of light.

Look at the children of Israel. When they tried to leave Satan's system in Egypt, Pharaoh resisted with all of his strength. Why do you suppose he didn't want them to leave? It was because he needed them to build his kingdom. Pharaoh didn't care about the Hebrews, and Satan doesn't care about people either. He is just using them to get access to the earth.

When we enter into the kingdom of God through salvation and are set free from Satan's bonds, sometimes we think great things will automatically happen for us. We believe blessings will come on us and overtake us. However, for those blessings to overtake us, we must hearken unto the voice of the Lord (Deut. 28:2). We need to lose confidence in the world's system and turn our attention fully to God and His Word, which contains the rules, or principles, of His kingdom.

GOD IS NOT MOVED BY NEED

The first principle of God's kingdom that we need to understand is that God is not moved by our need. Matthew 6:8 says,

Be not ye therefore like unto them: for your Father knoweth what things ye have need of, before ye ask him.

God knows what we need, but we must still ask Him. We must do something to have our needs met. If we don't do our part, God will not move on our behalf. There are many examples of this. In some parts of India, Africa, Haiti, and all over the world, people are starving to death. Why isn't God moving? It's because He is not moved by need.

What moves God? Jesus said many times, "O ye of little faith" (Matt. 6:30; 8:26; 16:8; Luke 12:28). The thing that moves God is faith. He designed His kingdom to work by faith in Him. We need faith to receive Him when we are born again and then to receive from Him from that point on.

When Elijah found the woman and her son in the middle of a famine, ready to eat their last meal, he didn't say, "You've survived all this time. Now I'm going to go out and get you some food." Rather, he said, "Sow some seed." If she hadn't sown some seed, expressing her faith in God, she and her son would have died that day (1 Kings 17). God is not moved by our need. He needs some seed that expresses our faith in Him.

It's not that God is mean. It's that He has set up His kingdom based on His wisdom, and we have to work within the principles of His kingdom. We don't have to go one more minute without our needs being met. We can work His system right now by first hearkening to the voice of the Lord and learning the principles of His kingdom from His Word.

The first principle, again, is that God is not moved by need. He is moved by faith. Somebody else can pray for us, and God will move on our behalf. God simply requires some faith from someone so that He can move. He said,

> *I sought for a man among them, that should make up the hedge, and stand in the gap before me for the land, that I should not destroy it: but I found none.*
>
> EZEKIEL 22:30

God wants to delay judgment on people who just don't know any better, but He needs somebody to stand in the gap to make up the hedge. He needs faith coming from someone on earth in order to work among us.

GOD WANTS TO SUPPLY OUR NEEDS

The second principle of God's kingdom that we need to understand to successfully operate in it is that God wants to supply our needs. He does not want any other thing or person or organization to be our source. He wants to be our source of supply.

In Exodus 20:2-3, God says,

I am the Lord thy God, which have brought thee out of the land of Egypt, out of the house of bondage. Thou shalt have no other gods before me.

This should eliminate all doubt that we brought ourselves into the kingdom of God. If you let some folks tell it, you'd think they saved themselves. However, our coming to Jesus was a work of God. God orchestrated it. Jesus said, "No man can come to me, except the Father which hath sent me draw him" (John 6:44).

After establishing that He saves us and delivers us, in Exodus God continues,

Thou shalt not make unto thee any graven image, or any likeness of any thing that is in heaven above, or that is in the earth beneath, or that is in the water under the earth. Thou shalt not bow down thyself to them, nor serve them: for I the Lord thy God am a jealous God.

                                                    Exodus 20:4-5

He called Himself a "jealous God." *The Living Bible* says, "I am very possessive." The *New Living Translation* says, "I will not share your affection with any other god." This sounds like a relationship.

If my wife came home one day and said, "Sweetheart, a man followed me into the store and bought me some shoes," I would be angry.

I'd say, "*Who* bought you *what?*" You could say I'm a jealous husband. I don't want anybody else making advances to my wife.

In the same way, we are the virgin fiancé of Jesus. He's espoused to us. He's taking care of us, and He wants to be our sole provider. He doesn't want anyone else taking care of His bride.

> *For we are members of his body, of his flesh, and of his bones. For this cause shall a man leave his father and mother, and shall be joined unto his wife, and they two shall be one flesh. This is a great mystery: but I speak concerning Christ and the church.*

EPHESIANS 5:30-32

Speaking of Jesus and the church, the Bible says we are bone of His bone and flesh of His flesh. That's a pretty intimate relationship! And our bridegroom loves us so much that He laid down His life for us. Of course, He wants to take good care of us! The psalmist wrote, "The Lord is my shepherd; I shall not want" (Ps 23:1). Jesus is our shepherd. He wants to meet all of our needs so that we do not want for anything—and He does not want us turning to any other shepherd.

God is a jealous God. We were never intended to be caught in an intimate relationship with the world's system. And Jesus doesn't want the world to take care of His bride. He says, "Don't touch her!" If we can catch that, then we will let go of the world's system, which is faithful to no one, and we will run to our faithful Lord. Lamentations 3:23 says, "Great is thy faithfulness." He is greatly faithful. Even when we are faithless, He's still faithful.

HOSEA AND HIS BRIDE: A PICTURE OF GOD AND HIS PEOPLE

In the book of Hosea, we read about the prophet by that name. God told him to marry a prostitute and said, "I'm going to show Israel what they're doing. They're running out on me with another god" (Hosea 1:2). Hosea married the prostitute, Gomer, and Israel watched as she left Hosea again and again to have sex with other men. She would be faithful for a while and then take off again. God was using Hosea to show Israel that He was a jealous husband who had been more than patient with her through her adulterous affairs with the world. He revealed His longsuffering toward them, but He also showed how miserable a life Gomer lived.

Living in victory in the kingdom of God requires faithfulness. It may not look like anything is happening, but no matter what we are seeing and hearing, we've got to stand and say, "My God shall supply all of my needs!" (Phil. 4:19). All we need is the Word of God, because the Word is our seed that expresses our faith in God, that we trust Him and Him alone.

He said, "Thou shalt not bow down thyself to [any other god]" (Ex. 20:5). Now, that's not a threat; that's a promise. That's God saying, "I'm going to take care of you."

Satan tried to get Jesus to worship him. He said, "Bow down, and I'll give you all you need." Satan is always trying to get people to worship him in exchange for getting their needs met. He stole that idea from God. As we worship and serve God, He meets all of our needs. That's how the kingdom of God works. Satan has patterned the kingdom of darkness after the kingdom of light. When people bow to him, he meets their need. But there is always destruction and death attached to it. That's why God commands us to stay away from the world's system. He knows that it will only cause us harm.

God said, "Do not bow down to any other god." We don't have to bow. We have Someone taking care of us who loves us. We didn't choose Him; He chose us. He picked us out. He saw us when we were down and out. Some of us didn't look so good! Our hair was all messed up, and we were so drunk that we didn't even know our own name. Some of us were smoking so much cocaine that our nose was about to wear out. Some of us had made some terrible mistakes, but none of that made any difference to God. He said, "I want you."

That's what it's all about. The story of Hosea illustrates this clearly. God said, "I'm married to the backslider. You've slid back on me, but I haven't slid back on you—because even when you are faithless, I am still faithful."

After Hosea married Gomer, she left Hosea. Even after having children with him, she went into the street, prostituting herself with other men. God told Hosea to go get her. She was probably beaten up, drugged, abused, and hurt, with no money or self-esteem left. But Hosea found her and said, "Come on. Let's go back home. I'm going to take you back just as you are." (See Hosea 3.)

That's what the kingdom of God is all about. No matter what our situation or condition, God takes us in. He wants us to be faithful to Him and Him alone. However, when we miss it and mess up, He is always waiting with open arms. And when we get a revelation of His incredible love for us, we never want to have anything to do with the world's system again. We want to look only to Him for everything we need in life.

SHADRACH, MESHACH, AND ABEDNEGO REFUSED TO BOW

Daniel tells the story of Shadrach, Meshach, and Abednego, who were supposed to bow down to worship the golden image of King Nebuchadnezzar. Daniel 3:14-15 says,

> *Nebuchadnezzar spake and said unto them, Is it true, O Shadrach, Meshach, and Abednego, do not ye serve my gods, nor worship the golden image which I have set up? Now if ye be ready that at what time ye hear the sound of the cornet, flute, harp, sackbut, psaltery, and dulcimer, and all kinds of musick, ye fall down and worship the image which I have made; well: but if ye worship not, ye shall be cast the same hour into the midst of a burning fiery furnace; and who is that God that shall deliver you out of my hands?*

The king was trying to make all people bow down and worship him. I think you know where he got that idea! Satan uses the world's system and those in it to try to make us bow to him and carry out his wishes. But the kingdom of God is in us and it rules over everything (Ps. 103). Shadrach, Meshach, and Abednego knew that.

Verses 16-17 continue,

> *Shadrach, Meshach, and Abednego, answered and said to the king, O Nebuchadnezzar, we are not careful to*

answer thee in this matter. If it be so, our God whom we serve is able to deliver us from the burning fiery furnace, and he will deliver us out of thine hand, O king.

When we believe in God enough to defy the world's pressures, God's system will work for us. He delivered Shadrach, Meshach, and Abednego from the fiery furnace. In fact, He showed up in the fire with them! Then they walked out of that fire not even smelling of smoke (Dan. 3:24-27). Just like these three faithful boys, God wants to supply all of our needs. He will when we depend on Him alone as Shadrach, Meshach, and Abednego did.

GOD MET ABRAM'S NEED

In Genesis 14 we find Abram's nephew Lot in trouble. Armies had come to take Sodom and Gomorrah and their king and all the other kings with them. They took Lot and all his goods and departed. When Abram found out about it, he took over three hundred trained servants to pursue, catch, and defeat them.

Verse 16 says,

And he brought back all the goods, and also brought again his brother Lot, and his goods, and the women also, and the people.

Abram and his men not only got the women, the men, and the children back, but they got the goods too.

The account continues,

And the king of Sodom went out to meet him after his return from the slaughter of Chedorlaomer, and of the kings that were with him, at the valley of Shaveh, which is the king's dale.

And the king of Sodom said unto Abram, Give me the persons, and take the goods to thyself.

And Abram said to the king of Sodom, I have lift up mine hand unto the Lord, the most high God, the possessor of heaven and earth, that I will not take from a thread even to a shoelatchet, and that I will not take any thing that is thine, lest thou shouldest say, I have made Abram rich.

GENESIS 14:17,21-23

Abram was following the rules of God's kingdom. He didn't want it to appear that anyone had made him rich but God, because God doesn't want anybody to say that they made His people rich. Almighty God is the One who will provide everything for us. Immediately after this, we see Abram receiving God's great promise.

After these things the word of the Lord came unto Abram in a vision, saying, Fear not, Abram: I am thy shield, and thy exceeding great reward. And Abram said, Lord God, what wilt thou give me, seeing I go childless, and the steward of my house is this Eliezer of Damascus? And Abram said, Behold, to me thou hast given no seed: and, lo, one born in my house is mine heir.

And, behold, the word of the Lord came unto him, saying, This shall not be thine heir; but he that shall come forth out of thine own bowels shall be thine heir. And he brought him forth abroad, and said, Look now toward heaven, and tell the stars, if thou be able to number them: and he said unto him, So shall thy seed be.

GENESIS 15:1-5

After years had passed and they still had no son, Sarai got out in front of God and tried to make her own way. Genesis 16:1-2 says,

Now Sarai Abram's wife bare him no children: and she had an handmaid, an Egyptian, whose name was Hagar. And Sarai said unto Abram, Behold now, the Lord hath restrained me from bearing.

Sarai assumed that God was restraining her from having a child, that He didn't want to supply her need—just Abram's. By contrast, when Hannah couldn't conceive, she made a vow to God, saying in essence, "If You give me a son, I'll give him back to You." The Bible says Hannah's womb opened after that. When we can't get any further, we have to go to the Word and ask the Holy Spirit to show us what we need to do to work within God's system. What seed do we need to plant? God is not trying to keep back our inheritance; He's waiting for us to plant some seed in faith.

Sarai continued in her own way, rather than finding God's way. She said to Abram,

I pray thee, go in unto my maid; it may be that I may obtain children by her. And Abram hearkened to the voice of Sarai. Abram listened to the wrong voice. He listened to Sarai instead of

God. He listened to the voice of the flesh instead of the voice of the Spirit.

And Sarai Abram's wife took Hagar her maid the Egyptian, after Abram had dwelt ten years in the land of Canaan, and gave her to her husband Abram to be his wife.

GENESIS 16:3

Sarai gave Hagar to Abram so that she could have a child, but that wasn't what God had promised. She was trying to do it her own way instead of waiting on God. Sometimes God's way takes a little bit longer, and what we have to do is wait on Him. If God promised, He's faithful to perform it.

Hagar had Abram's child, and his name was Ishmael. Because Abram and Sarai hadn't trusted God, they made a plan outside of God's plan. As a result, a great division of people began, a division between Arab (Ishmael) and Jew (Isaac) that remains today.

If we absolutely trust God, we're at peace. When we know how it's going to turn out, we don't get anxious for anything. However, when we get anxious, we try to act on our own behalf and make messes that only God can clean up. Therefore, in the end we always turn to Him anyway! God told Abram, "Your name will no longer be Abram, but now it will be Abraham." In a spiritual sense, He was marrying Abram and giving him a new name. He promised Abraham, "I will be your God." (See Genesis 17.) Finally, when Abraham was ninety-nine and Sarah was ninety, they had their son, Isaac.

GOD GETS THE GLORY

God meets our need through our seeds of faith in Him and His Word. He doesn't want us to figure out how to meet our need by the flesh or our carnal thinking. He wants to meet our need and give us the revelation of it in the Spirit. Then, every time our needs are met, He is glorified.

Satan is always trying to get the glory from God's people. He wants to meet our need through carnal means and then pull the rug out from under us later. But God wants to meet all our need according to His riches in glory by Christ Jesus (Phil. 4:19). That means He gets the glory and we get blessed and more blessed. He never comes back later to harm us as Satan does.

God kept working with Abraham, and Abraham became the father of many nations. God will keep working with us as well. He can turn around the messes we make when we pursue things our own way, but it's better for us to not have gone our way at all. When we work according to the principles of God's kingdom and depend on Him alone, He will meet all of our need and get all the glory.

Most people don't have a problem with prosperity, but some people have a problem with God providing it. If they can say they did it themselves, it makes them feel good. They will work three jobs to make it, doing it all in their own thinking and strength, just so they can say that they got the victory in the end. They have no understanding of God's grace.

First of all, if God did lead a believer to take three jobs, He would supply the strength and wisdom they needed to do them.

When the victory came, all the glory would go to Him. But many times believers will be like Sarai and do things the hard way. They get into their own thinking and strength when God has a way of His grace for them to get the victory.

God simply wants us to know that He is the One who provides for us. When I lay hands on the sick, God proves He's the One who heals them. One time I was praying for a man who'd been in a domestic fight and had a knife wound all the way down his arm. He couldn't even move his hand. The power of God hit him, and he started moving his hand. With tears running down his face, he said, "Look, I can move my hand!" There was a new believer from the projects who had just been delivered of alcoholism helping me at the time. He stepped out and said, "Well, shake my hand then. Shake my hand!" This new believer jumped in with both feet. He shook this man's hand, and it was as whole as ever.

Both of these men knew that I didn't make that happen. We don't perform the miracle; the Living Word does. Our job is to plant the seed, and God's job is to meet the need. And when He meets the need, He gets all the glory.

THE FIRST SEED IS GOD'S WORD

As we have seen before, we express our faith in God and God alone by believing His Word. The first seed that we plant for every need we have is the Word of God. We have to get God's Word on everything we want to do before God can come in and do it because He is looking for faith. And we know that faith comes "by hearing, and hearing by the Word of God" (Rom. 10:17).

The Word changes our image of ourselves and God. It changes what we believe, causing faith to rise up and believe in Him. And God can only work with us to the degree that we believe in Him. Mark 4:14 says, "The sower soweth the word" because we have to sow the Word in our hearts in order to have faith in God. It is our responsibility to sow. If we don't sow anything, we don't reap anything.

Mark 4:26-27 says,

> *So is the kingdom of God, as if a man should cast seed into the ground; and should sleep, and rise night and day, and the seed should spring and grow up, he knoweth not how.*

The seed will spring up and grow, even if we don't know how. We don't need to try to figure out the details. When we're dealing with God, we can leave the details out. God just has us to do things. He said, "In the name of Jesus lay hands on the sick, and they shall recover" (Mark 16:18). "In the name of Jesus speak to the mountain, and it shall move" (Mark 11:23.)

He didn't say, "Inquire about it. Ask, 'How's this mountain going to move?'" In Matthew 21, Jesus didn't come up to the fig tree and say, "Now, what kind of tree is this? How big is this tree? Bring the tape measure over here, and let's just go around. Let's see. What kind of root system is that?" No, He didn't care about anything but the fruit. He cursed the tree because there was no fruit. We don't need the details to bear fruit for the kingdom of God. Once we get the revelation knowledge from God's Word that we need, God takes care of the rest.

The enemy's job is to get us into details so he can get us into the intellect and our own thinking. If he gets us into our carnal thinking, we are no longer in the spirit or operating in faith toward God. That's why we have to stay in the spirit. When we stay in the spirit, sometimes we will move at a pace that our mind won't be able to calculate. We will move at the speed of the spirit, not the speed of the carnal mind.

Mark 4:28-29 says,

> *For the earth bringeth forth fruit of herself; first the blade, then the ear, after that the full corn in the ear. But when the fruit is brought forth, immediately he putteth in the sickle, because the harvest is come.*

When revelation and light break through in our hearts, if we don't act on the Word of God, Satan will come and try to steal that revelation. So when we find out that God wants to provide for all of our needs and that we need to sow some seed, we need to get to sowing! We can't wait to check things out or get caught up in the details. If we wait too long, that light will start growing dim because we are not really trusting in God but in our own ability.

THE KINGDOM WORKING IN US

When I was a manager at work, the economy took a big nose-dive. All the managers at my job got together and started having a big pity party, talking about how bad things were. Then out of my heart I heard, "Why don't you do what you've been learning about?" That was the Word in me. I had sown it in my heart, and now it was starting to talk to me. When we plant the Word in our heart, we'll start getting messages in our mind that we didn't think of. That's the kingdom working in us.

After the meeting that morning I went to my office, and the phone rang. It was my sister. She knew that business was bad. I said, "You call me at five o'clock this afternoon, and I'll have more business than I can put on the books." That sure wasn't my mind talking because this was the last day of the month, and I had to produce to feed my family. Once I said that, that word that was conceived in the soil of my heart went to work. The same happened for Peter when he launched out and pulled in a boat-sinking, net-breaking load of fish. The kingdom of God is the production center for the Word we confess. The kingdom was now working to bring to pass what I had said. Out of the abundance of the heart the mouth speaks, and a good tree brings forth good fruit.

My salespeople were out in their territories trying to get me some business, and at about twelve o'clock they began to call in. "Hey, Bill, this guy just gave me an order for a large computer." They were making sales all over the place, and before five o'clock I started putting the sales on the books.

My boss said, "Wait a minute! This is too much! Let's save some of this for next month." He thought next month was going to be a drought too, but the next month the same thing happened. There was enough business to cover that whole branch. It covered the other managers who were short. God doesn't bring us a little; He doesn't know anything about "a little." He's the God of abundance. He always has more than enough. That's the way we can find His fingerprint.

Instead of letting the world's system work us, why don't we start working God's system? There is a hidden system inside of us. It's set up to produce for us if we follow God's principles. It's designed to create for us, bring us to, or bring to us everything we need in this earth—independent of what's going on around us. That is the gospel of the kingdom of God.

The moment we have a need that can't be met, we just need to work the principles of the kingdom of God. Mark 4:14 says, "The sower soweth the word." Some of us have been tolerating things that we could overcome if we would just work God's system. Remember: He that promised is faithful to do it. Our deliverance comes out of our spirit, from the inside out, not from the outside in. God is faithful, and when we switch from the kingdom of darkness to the kingdom of light, He will provide our every need according to His riches in glory by Christ Jesus. All we need to do is plant our seeds of faith, watch Him bring forth the fruit we need, and then give Him all the glory.

CHAPTER 9

SWITCHING SYSTEMS: CONFRONTING THE WORLD'S PHILOSOPHIES WITH GOD'S TRUTH

As we switch from the system of the world to the system of God's kingdom, we have to learn to identify the deception of the enemy that has infiltrated the church. The only way we can do that is to discover God's truth about His will for us. We find His truth in His Word. In Matthew 6:9-13 Jesus identifies the truth.

> *After this manner therefore pray ye: Our Father which art in heaven, Hallowed be thy name. Thy kingdom come, Thy will be done in earth, as it is in heaven. Give us this day our daily bread. And forgive us our debts, as*

we forgive our debtors. And lead us not into temptation, but deliver us from evil: For thine is the kingdom, and the power, and the glory, for ever. Amen.

When Jesus says, "Our Father," that tells us that we're to relate to God as Daddy. Daddy is the One we look to for our provision, our guidance, our teaching—for everything.

When He says, "Hallowed be thy name," it tells us that we're to reverence God's name. We're also to reverence His Word. That Word is not just some word; it's God's Word. We're to take God's Word as the absolute truth.

When He says, "Thy kingdom come, Thy will be done in earth, as it is in heaven," it shows us that God still wants the earth to be like heaven. Jesus told us to pray like this. He showed us that God's will is for the earth to be like heaven and that He will allow what we'll allow by the words of our mouths—our prayers.

Right away, many people will take exception to that. However, all we have to do is turn back to the book of Genesis and look at Adam. Did God allow Adam to sin? God told him, "Don't do it," but Adam did it. (See Genesis 2.) God allowed what Adam allowed, and He will allow what we allow. As a matter of fact, He is allowing what believers allow right now. He's given us authority over this earth. To touch the earth that He gave to humankind, He needs our permission. We give Him that permission through prayer and our confession.

If we want to be broke and poor, He'll allow it. His will is that we prosper and be in health as our soul prospers (3 John 2.) His will is that wealth and riches be in our house because our soul is at peace with Him (Ps. 112:3). However, as long as we let those blessings sit in heaven because we are not at peace with Him by abiding in His Word, He'll let our blessings sit there. God will allow us to be sick, broke, in a troubled marriage, or even to die before our time because He'll allow anything we'll allow. If we don't get God involved in it, He'll just stand back and allow it.

We can't blame God and think He's being mean or that He's our problem. Job tried that. He set up a system and an order, and we have to cooperate with that system to receive what He has given us through the redemption of Jesus Christ.

In the Garden of Eden, God said, "Let us make man in our image, after our likeness: and let them have dominion" (Gen. 1:26). *Dominion* means "supreme authority; absolute owner-ship."[1] It means you are in charge. God didn't have dominion over the earth then, and He still doesn't have it. Since Adam, human beings have always had dominion, which is why the devil wanted to become their spiritual head. Then he could get access to the earth and set up his own kingdom through man. The truth is, Satan doesn't really have much power. What he's using is the power still resident in fallen man to do his damage.

When Jesus paid the price for sin and took the keys of death and hell from Satan, He made a way for people to be reconciled to God and come under His headship again. The Son of God had to pay the price for sin and to bring God's Spirit and pres-ence back into the lives of human beings as a man.

After the resurrection, Jesus provided reconciliation to God for all human beings who wanted Him. And when Jesus becomes their Savior and Lord, the kingdom of God dwells within them.

Now, instead of exercising their dominion under the influence of Satan, giving him access to the earth and all its resources, the people of God exercise their dominion under the lordship of Jesus Christ, bringing the presence and power of God into the earth.

Jesus gave us all authority in His name (Matt. 16:19) because He was going to be seated at the right hand of the Father (Mark 16:19). He gave it to us because we're in the earth, and He wanted us to exercise dominion over the earth with all the power of heaven behind us. Once we understand this, we will find ourselves praying and exercising our dominion in the full authority of God and His Word. One of the main reasons people don't pray is that for some reason they think things will automatically happen. They say, "Oh, God knows what we need." Yes, He knows, but He is waiting for us to express our faith by praying His Word and will into the earth. He wants us to be in health, but if someone is terminally ill with no medical cure and no one prays in faith, He will allow us to die. He wants to bless us financially, but if we never pray His Word over our job in faith, He has nothing to work with.

I want to make this so plain that we have no problem praying. It is shameful when the church doesn't want to pray. God will allow our neighborhoods to be run over. He'll allow drugs and gangs to come in and harm our children and steal our cars. Whatever we allow, He allows—good or bad.

THE BLIND LEADING THE BLIND

See to it that no one carries you off as spoil or makes you yourselves captive by his so-called philosophy and intellectualism and vain deceit (idle fancies and plain

130

nonsense), following human tradition (men's ideas of the material rather than the spiritual world), just crude notions following the rudimentary and elemental teachings of the universe and disregarding [the teachings of] Christ (the Messiah).

COLOSSIANS 2:8 AMP

We've had ignorant teaching, and in some cases no teaching, about the kingdom of God. We've had the blind leading the blind, and the devil has walked all over us because of it. I'm fed up with playing games with the enemy. It's time for us to understand how God's system works and confront the world's philosophies so that we can live in the "abundant life" He offers us, and His presence and power will cover the whole earth.

We Die Once

One wrong philosophy that we've had in the church comes from Ecclesiastes 3:1-2, which says,

To every thing there is a season, and a time to every purpose under the heaven: A time to be born, and a time to die.

Some leaders have preached that God has a set time for every person to die, and now people think that God took some little baby or some teenager because it was the "appointed time" for them to die. That is not scriptural.

Hebrews 9:27-28 repeats the message, but in a different way.

And as it is appointed unto men once to die, but after this the judgment: so Christ was once offered to bear the

sins of many; and unto them that look for him shall he appear the second time without sin unto salvation.

It says it is appointed to men once to die. In other words, every human being must die once. However, it does not say there is a predetermined time for each person to die or that God comes and indiscriminately kills us. Consider Jairus's daughter and Lazarus, who both died and were raised from the dead. Obviously, God did not set a time for them to die. We know that eventually they died and went to heaven, but in the end, the time of their death was between them and God. Everything we do in life—and death—is (or should be) a decision we make with God. Again, what we allow in our lives is what God allows.

This verse also addresses reincarnation. It is saying that people don't live and die and then live again as a cow or rat, then die and live again as something else on earth. People live their lives on earth once and die. They don't come back again into this earth either as people, animals, or anything else. After they die, they either go to heaven or hell. "And as it is appointed unto men once to die, *but after this the judgment*" will determine where you and I will spend eternity.

Ecclesiastes is just saying that everyone will die someday, and Hebrews is saying it is appointed to every person to die at least once (considering that they might be raised from the dead if they die). Neither of these verses say that there is a specific time when God will cause a person to die. God is not the author of death; Satan is. (See 1 Corinthians 15:25-26 and John 10:10.) Study how the patriarchs of old died: Abraham, Isaac, and Jacob.

We have to spend time in the Word and in prayer to grasp the gospel of the kingdom. Otherwise, the enemy will take a misunderstanding of the Scripture to try to snuff out a person's life before that person has accomplished their divine destiny and purpose. Then the devil will have the victory at a funeral as some preacher talks about the Lord "plucking up this young one like a little flower because He needed him in heaven!" That is the blind leading the blind. When Job said that the Lord gave and the Lord had taken away, it was truly stated but not a statement of truth. The devil was the agent that destroyed Job's business and took his kids' lives (Job 1:21). In the last chapter, Job got back twofold what he lost.

God Is Good and He Loves You

The enemy has been able to infiltrate people's lives because religious thinking and condemnation put them in a position of non-resistance. He tells us that God is making us suffer because He is trying to teach us something. That kind of reasoning will get a person killed, and that's exactly what the enemy wants.

The devil's accusations are an insult to God's character. The Father has gone to such great lengths for us. He sent His Son to die for us and take all the sickness and disease, the suffering, the pain, the shame, and the unrighteousness of mankind on Himself. When people believe they're just a worm in the dust or that God hasn't forgiven them for some former sin, they couldn't be further from the truth. God sent Jesus to bear our sins and carry our diseases because He loves us and values our lives. He wants us well and able to serve Him.

Then there is the common philosophy that God uses evil things to teach us. Jesus said, "Lead us *not* into temptation" (Matt. 6:13, emphasis added). We're not supposed to be praying, "Lord, please lead me into some more testing. I need to be tested just a little bit more." A statement like that will cause a miscarriage of God's justice because Jesus suffered for us. The suffering that we do is the suffering of standing on the Word. As we stand on the Word, sometimes the enemy comes against us and tempts us with evil. Sometimes he sends people to persecute us. However, God doesn't want us to suffer something evil, such as adultery, just to teach us something. That's the devil trying to destroy our lives!

When we are delivered from the kingdom of darkness to the kingdom of light, we need to understand that God is a good God who loves us like a good father loves his children. The enemy will try to bring us under condemnation or tell us that we're an exception, but let's not let him talk us out of it! Let's get into the Word, find out the truth, and believe it.

If we want to know what God is like, we just have to look at Jesus. Jesus said that when you see Him, you see the Father (John 14:9). If we study Jesus we will better understand God. Jesus told us the truth, healed us, delivered us from demons, forgave us, and loved us so much that He died a cruel death so we could be with Him forever. His life illustrated the character and nature of our God, who is love personified.

The Bible Tells Us the Truth

The Bible gives us the gospel of the kingdom, and the gospel of the kingdom is a report of everything available to us in earth and in heaven. The Bible is basically a copy of everything that Jesus left to us in the will after His death and resurrection. It's ours. This is the truth, and we have to renew our minds to it. We aren't under the law of the Old Testament; we're under the grace of God in the New Testament. We have a whole new system of relationship with God. In the Old Testament, the Holy Spirit came upon only the prophet, priest, or king to speak to all the people. In the New Testament, we have the Holy Spirit living inside of each one of us (John 14:16,17). He stands with us and intercedes for us (Rom. 8:26.)

In the Old Testament God's people didn't have the Redeemer or a heavenly High Priest. They had a natural high priest, but he failed sometimes. In the New Testament Jesus is our Redeemer and High Priest forever, and He never fails.

All of this truth and more is found in the Bible! We can't let the enemy keep us in darkness. He wants to keep us ignorant of God and His kingdom so that he can move into our lives through his deception and lies. However, if we know the truth of God's Word, we can stop him in his tracks and fulfill our divine destiny. Every time we receive revelation from God's Word and respond to it, we switch another area of our lives from the kingdom of darkness to the kingdom of God.

REAL PROSPERITY

Another area where there is misunderstanding in the church is prosperity. Jesus taught us how to distinguish between the wealth of the world and the wealth of the kingdom. Luke 12:22-24,30 says,

And he said unto his disciples, Therefore I say unto you, Take no thought for your life, what ye shall eat; neither for the body, what ye shall put on. The life is more than meat, and the body is more than raiment. Consider the ravens: for they neither sow nor reap; which neither have storehouse nor barn; and God feedeth them: how much more are ye better than the fowls?...For all these things do the nations of the world seek after: and your Father knoweth that ye have need of these things.

We try to store up a lot, but then we begin to trust in that visible storage. God isn't against savings accounts, but He doesn't want our trust to be in our savings accounts. He wants us to trust Him and Him alone for all of our needs.

Jesus demonstrated to the disciples that we can have what we need anytime we need it without carrying it around in our pockets. The system of prosperity in the kingdom of God works similar to how we use a personal check in some societies. We have a need and just write a check for it. That amount of money is taken out of our bank account to pay for the goods or services we have purchased with the check. Real prosperity is the ability to use God's heavenly ability to meet any earthly need that we may have anytime, on any level (spirit, soul, body, social, or financial) independent of the circumstances. Instead of a personal check, however, we use the Word of God in our hearts and by faith declare God's will for our lives. We sow from the spirit to reap in the natural.

When the disciples needed food for themselves and for thousands of other people, God provided through Jesus, the

Living Word. A little boy sowed his two fish and five loaves, and then Jesus sowed it by lifting it to God in thanks and distributing it to the disciples. That seed was sown twice. Jesus then received the increase, and through that increase He fed everybody. (See John 6:5-13.) Jesus was teaching them that what we see is not all there is. There is an invisible, inexhaustible heavenly supply.

This is the mystery of the kingdom of God, something beyond human comprehension. If we get our mind renewed with the truth of God's Word, our spirit will tell us what is really going on. Then, anytime our spirit and our senses conflict, we need to go the way of our spirit. The results are that we'll find there is no shortage. In the natural, you may perceive a shortage, but in reality there is no shortage in the spirit according to God's Word.

Our intellect cannot receive this. Only revelation knowledge can take you beyond your intellect and matter. This is not a function of the carnal mind because, as Jesus told us, His Word is spirit and life. Spiritual truth can only be processed by a spirit being. The kingdom of God has come inside us by the Holy Spirit, and it is there to provide everything we need without our going to the system of the world. That's why the Bible says, "The kingdom of God is not meat and drink; but righteousness, and peace, and joy in the Holy Ghost" (Rom. 14:17).

The kingdom of God is a new government for the individual believer and the church, and with that government comes everything that we need individually and corporately. It will provide joy for us when everyone around us is crying, peace when the world is fearful, and love when there is hatred all around.

Ephesians 1:2-3 says,

Grace be to you, and peace, from God our Father, and from the Lord Jesus Christ. Blessed be the God and Father of our Lord Jesus Christ, who hath blessed us with all spiritual blessings in heavenly places in Christ.

God has blessed us with all spiritual blessings in Christ Jesus. In Him God has supplied every need that we have while we're living on this earth. It's all in heavenly places in Christ— the Anointed One—and comes to us through His Anointing, the Holy Ghost.

The next verse says,

According as he hath chosen us in him before the foundation of the world.
EPHESIANS 1:4

We were chosen in Him and our spiritual blessings were placed in Him before the foundation of the world. The moment God had us in mind He set aside everything we would need. In the mind of God, we are everything He made us to be right now. He sees Jesus in us and us in Jesus now. We are without a spot or wrinkle in His eyes right now. All of heaven's provisions are ours now. Verse 11 says, "In whom also we have obtained an inheritance." In Jesus Christ we have already inherited everything we need. That is *real prosperity!*

BEWARE THE LEAVEN OF PHARISEES
AND SADDUCEES

The kingdom of God is the government of God, so when we are born again we are switching from the government of this world to the government of God. We're switching from external religious rules to God's laws of the kingdom written in our heart (spirit). Jesus instructs His disciples to distinguish between these two systems in Matthew 16:5-6, when He says,

> *And when his disciples were come to the other side, they*
> *had forgotten to take bread. Then Jesus said unto them,*
> *Take heed and beware of the leaven of the Pharisees and*
> *of the Sadducees.*

The Pharisees were hypocritical and legalistic; and when it came down to it, they weren't even keeping the rules they made. They were putting heavy burdens on everybody else, burdens that they weren't even carrying. They knew they were falling short, but they didn't act like it. They were hypocrites, who appeared very holy on the outside, but inwardly Jesus said they were like dead men's bones (Matt. 23:27.)

The Sadducees claimed a higher enlightenment. They were led by their intellect, but the human mind was never meant to lead us. God created us to be led by the Holy Spirit in our spirits. Our minds were meant to follow our spirits.

Matthew 16:7 shows that the disciples reacted to Jesus' warning with their minds instead of their spirits.

> *And they reasoned among themselves, saying, It is*
> *because we have taken no bread.*

The disciples were using their natural reasoning and assumed Jesus was talking about natural leaven, which is yeast. They said, essentially, "He's talking about yeast because we forgot to bring bread." Watch what Jesus does.

> *Which when Jesus perceived, he said unto them, O ye of little faith, why reason ye among yourselves, because ye have brought no bread? Do ye not yet understand, neither remember the five loaves of the five thousand, and how many baskets ye took up? Neither the seven loaves of the four thousand, and how many baskets ye took up?*
>
> *How is it that ye do not understand that I spake it not to you concerning bread, that ye should beware of the leaven of the Pharisees and of the Sadducees? Then understood they how that he bade them not beware of the leaven of bread, but of the doctrine of the Pharisees and of the Sadducees.*
>
> MATTHEW 16:8-12

First, Jesus deals with their natural concern that they have no bread to eat. He reminds them how He had worked God's system to feed the multitudes. The kingdom had produced not only enough for Him and His disciples but for thousands. And He points out how quickly they had forgotten the truth, gotten back into fear, looking to the natural realm to supply their needs instead of God. Then Jesus addresses the spiritual truth He was giving them, that the leaven of the Sadducees and Pharisees was their doctrine. Religious people will teach rules and law, which are generally tied to the world's system. Obviously, that is not sound doctrine or good teaching!

The Pharisees and the Sadducees didn't understand faith, grace, or any other principle of the kingdom of God because their salvation was based on their own good works and behavior instead of the work of Jesus Christ. That is why Jesus said to beware of their teaching. They were incapable of understanding that there is no condemnation in the kingdom of God. His grace provides forgiveness and restoration whenever we sin or break His laws. However, we no longer want to break His laws, and we will not break His laws if we live by the Spirit of life in Christ Jesus.

> *There is therefore now no condemnation to them which are in Christ Jesus, who walk not after the flesh, but after the Spirit. For the law of the Spirit of life in Christ Jesus hath made me free from the law of sin and death.*
>
> ROMANS 8:1-2

SOWING AND REAPING: THE PLATFORM OF KINGDOM PRINCIPLES

In the parable of the sower in Mark, chapter 4, Jesus gives an illustration of how the Word of God is planted in the heart by comparing it with seed sown in the ground. Jesus tells us that the parable of sowing and reaping is the very platform by which all of the other principles of the kingdom work.

> *Know ye not this parable? and how then will ye know all parables? The sower soweth the word.*
>
> MARK 4:13-14

In Luke 8:11 Jesus says, "The seed is the word of God."

The Word of God is the seed we plant to get a harvest of blessings in the kingdom of God. The sower sows the Word seed, and that Word seed controls everything. When God said, "Let there be light" (Gen. 1:3), the environment changed because of His Word. The Word establishes, forms, and changes the natural world around us. Everything in our lives must either line up or get out when we stand on the Word. That's how powerful it is.

Even when it looks as though it's not working, we have to stand on God's Word. When we've done all we can do to stand, the Bible says we just have to stand (Eph. 6:13). We have to keep confessing, keep declaring, keep proclaiming, and keep saying the Word because that is God's will for our lives.

People tend to give up because they think it's not working, but everything has to yield to the Word. If we plant the Word seed and cover it with cement, it will still come up. It will break a hole in the pavement to do what God says. Everything must submit to the authority and power of the Word of God.

Spiritual truth is always under demonic attack, so if we don't practice it or rehearse it in our minds, we'll be just like the disciples. The devil will come in and steal what once was a part of our way of doing things. We'll find "the cares of this world, the deceitfulness of riches, and the desires of other things" will enter in, choking the Word and making it unfruitful in our lives (Mark 4:19).

When we focus on the world more than on the kingdom of God, Jesus said it will be hard to get the revelation of what the Word says because our eyes are set on the kingdom of darkness.

The light of the body is the eye: if therefore thine eye be single, thy whole body shall be full of light. But if thine eye be evil, thy whole body shall be full of darkness. If therefore the light that is in thee be darkness, how great is that darkness! No man can serve two masters: for either he will hate the one, and love the other; or else he will hold to the one, and despise the other.

MATTHEW 6:22-24

If we put our entire attention on the Word of God rather than the world, then our eye will be "single" and our "whole body will be full of light." That means we will get illumination from God that can come from no other source. Our ties with the world, and putting our attention on the world, can cause worry, greed, lust, and more faith in the natural world than in God. The enemy tries to get us to care, complain, and worry about things so that we will negate the effect of the Word of God that has been sown in our hearts.

One of the things that is acceptable in the world but greatly unacceptable with God is worry and complaining. People in the world and even some believers don't mind if you get upset and complain, but God can't stand it. Those complainers in the time of the Exodus stayed right where they were in the wilderness for forty years because of worry and complaining.

God wants us to be full of faith in Him and His Word and carefree. If we have a worry, He wants us to cast that thing over on Him because He will care for us (1 Pet. 5:7). He's our Father, and He loves us more than anyone in the world can love us.

No matter how bad it looks, what the doctor just said, what the children just did, or what the money situation looks like, we are not to worry. When we worry, we open the door to the enemy. Then when he comes in, he tries to negate whatever promises God has given us. He tries to tell us that God doesn't want to bless us. But God's will hasn't changed. He always wants us to be healthy; He always wants our children to follow Him; He always wants us to have more than enough. We just got worried. We must take heed not to worry but instead put the Word first and see ourselves receiving God's blessing. Then the Word in us will not be choked, and what we have sown will bear fruit in our lives.

In Luke 21:26, Jesus says that in the last days men's hearts will fail them for fear. He's not necessarily talking about people having heart attacks, even though that may happen; He's talking about people's hearts failing to produce what they need because of fear. Fear will stop faith, and faith is what we need for the kingdom to produce.

God is lavish, and He produces lavishly. Mark 4:20 says that when we "hear the word, and receive it," we "bring forth fruit, some thirtyfold, some sixty, and some an hundred." Notice it says that we hear the Word, not CNN or ABC. That's why Jesus said, "Take heed what ye hear" (v. 24). We can't hear (listen to) everything. We have to choose not to hear things that cause our hearts to stop producing.

What we need to do is continually plant the seed of the Word in our hearts. Jesus said,

> *So is the kingdom of God, as if a man should cast seed into the ground; and should sleep, and rise night and*

day, and the seed should spring and grow up, he knoweth not how. For the earth bringeth forth fruit of herself; first the blade, then the ear, after that the full corn in the ear. But when the fruit is brought forth, immediately he putteth in the sickle, because the harvest is come.

MARK 4:26-29

Just as it is vital that we plant Word seeds, it is vital that we harvest them. If we sow the Word and receive it in our heart soil, but then we fail to act on it at harvest time when it is fully developed, the enemy will steal that Word from us. That Word will be ineffective in our lives.

In verses 30-32 Jesus continues,

Whereunto shall we liken the kingdom of God? or with what comparison shall we compare it? It is like a grain of mustard seed, which, when it is sown in the earth, is less than all the seeds that be in the earth: but when it is sown, it groweth up, and becometh greater than all herbs, and shooteth out great branches; so that the fowls of the air may lodge under the shadow of it.

God is a supernatural provider, and He provides for us as we express our faith in Him and His Word. He doesn't want us to say just anything. He wants us to sow the Word, to think and speak what He thinks and says, and then He'll multiply it back to us so that it provides not only for us and our families but for thousands.

The Bible makes it clear that speaking God's Word is powerful. All increase and decrease come by the tongue because what you say is what you sow. Proverbs 18:20 says, "A man's belly shall be satisfied with the fruit of his mouth; and with the increase of his lips shall he be filled."

Psalm 50:23 says,

> *Whoso offereth praise glorifieth me: and to him that ordereth his conversation aright will I shew the salvation of God.*

Salvation, prosperity, healing, and all increase come by the Word seed that we plant in our hearts, in our lives, and in the people and situations around us.

GOD WANTS US TO STAY IN THE KINGDOM

God not only wants us to come out of the kingdom of darkness, but He wants us to stay out. He doesn't want us to give glory to anybody else, follow anybody else, or worship anybody else but Him. He wants us to come into His kingdom and keep doing things His way from now on in spirit, soul, and body.

When the devil tempted Jesus, saying, "If thou therefore wilt worship me, all shall be thine," Jesus said, "Get thee behind me, Satan: for it is written, Thou shalt worship the Lord thy God, and him only shalt thou serve" (Luke 4:8). God wants us to see clearly the temptations of the devil to depend on the world's system instead of Him. That is why He wants us to worship and serve Him alone. He wants us to see who He is and who we are in Him. This is not so He can hold us captive but so that He can keep us safe and satisfied.

The world's system programmed an ungodly, evil self-image inside of each of us. When we come out of the world, God proceeds to get that unholy self-image from the world out of us.

He's changing the image on the inside because we can't switch systems on the outside if we haven't switched systems on the inside. We must see and understand who we are in Christ Jesus inside to be like Jesus on the outside.

Once we switch systems on the inside and begin to see and understand who we are in Christ Jesus, we can begin to operate in the system of God's kingdom and obey Jesus' directive to occupy the earth till He comes. We can fulfill our divine destiny in Him.

SWITCHING SYSTEMS

When we speak about switching systems, we mean moving from the current Babylonian system of buying and selling to God's kingdom system of sowing and reaping. Increase in the kingdom of God doesn't come by what you sell, but it is based on what you sow. And increase will only result from seed sown.

An illustration of this is found in Genesis 26, when Isaac sowed in a land and time of famine and received in the same year one hundredfold in return. The Lord blessed him, and he became very rich. He became so rich that the Philistine government asked him to leave the country!

Another example is the woman in 2 Kings, chapter 4, whose two sons were about to be enslaved to pay off the family debt. She cried to Elisha, and he asked her what she had in the house. She replied, "Thine handmaiden hath not any thing in the house, save a pot of oil." I've heard some preachers say that this was burial oil, which was extremely expensive. It had the value of a year's wages.[2] The prophet directed her to get empty vessels and to pour the oil into them, or sow the oil. Out of her obedience she experienced a miracle. The oil was multiplied by God and filled all the vessels which were limited only by her faith. Elisha then directed her to sell the oil. With the money she received for the oil she could pay the debt, and she and her family would live on the rest.

The same principle of sowing and reaping works in the New Testament. In Luke, chapter 5, Peter had fished all night and caught nothing, but when he sowed his boat into Jesus' ministry, he received a miracle catch. There were so many fish that he couldn't contain them in the net.

Unfortunately, many believers today are either unaware of God's system of sowing and reaping or heard it and refused to believe it or walk in it. Some are like the rich young ruler in Luke 18:18-25, who asked Jesus, "What shall I do to inherit eternal life?" Jesus told him to go and sell what he had and give the money to the poor. Then he would have treasure in heaven. The rich man was sad at this saying and went away grieved. He lacked the revelation of the system of sowing and reaping, and he was overtaken by fear of loss. He did not obey Jesus and missed a great opportunity for increase, as well as service to our Lord.

Another example of God's system at work is in Genesis, chapter 30, when Jacob worked for his father-in-law, Laban. Laban changed Jacob's wages ten times, and in the natural it looked like Jacob would never make enough money to have his own and to support his family. But God gave Jacob a dream, and when Jacob obeyed God's instructions in the dream and worked the system God's way, all of Laban's wealth was transferred into Jacob's hands. Jacob switched from a payday system of seeing his salary or Laban as his source to God's system of sowing and reaping. He took charge of his own financial destiny by trusting God and doing things God's way. As a result, God blessed him greatly.

If you are waiting on payday, I encourage you to switch from the system of this world to the system of the kingdom of God. You will soon see how payday can be every day! All of these biblical accounts illustrate that whatever increase you need begins with the Word of God and sowing what He leads you to sow.

Switching systems involves being ruled by the Word of God in our hearts rather than the external systems or conditions in the world. It involves going from information, or intellectual knowledge received by way of the five senses, to revelation knowledge received directly from God. Proverbs 20:27 says, "The spirit of man is the candle of the Lord, searching all the inward parts of the belly." What this means is that God uses your spirit to guide you. The way Jesus was one step ahead of the devil and his strategies was that he received information from God in His spirit. When the multitudes were hungry, Jesus knew in His spirit what His Father wanted Him to do to feed them.

In switching systems, you are going from a paycheck mentality to an abundance mentality, from a natural expectancy to a supernatural expectancy. You are switching from trusting in yourself and natural things to trusting in God and His miracle-producing Word. And most important, you are doing the same thing Jesus did when He faced the challenges and problems of life on earth—living by faith in God and in His Word to supply every need.

God designed a system in the earth in you, in every believer, that will produce everything you need independent of your environment. Switching systems involves looking to your spirit, the Holy Spirit, and God's Word to produce what you need supernaturally. Your spirit is the ground in which you deposit the miraculous seed of the Word of God. Then out of that seed good things and miraculous things will grow.

God honors His Word planted in faith, and He will cause the increase by supernaturally overriding the natural circumstances. I've found that people don't have a problem with prosperity. They just have a problem with God doing it. They cannot or will not trust Him to prosper them regardless of their situation. As you trust in God and His Word, however, the kingdom of God inside of you is designed to produce for you everything you have need of in this earth *in abundance.* You can literally tap into an inexhaustible supply from heaven and live like heaven upon the earth. All you need to do is switch from the world's system to God's system!

CHAPTER 10

OCCUPYING THE EARTH
TILL JESUS COMES

In Luke 19:12-13, Jesus says,

> *A certain nobleman went into a far country to receive*
> *for himself a kingdom, and to return. And he called his*
> *ten servants, and delivered them ten pounds, and said*
> *unto them, Occupy till I come.*

When Jesus said, "Occupy until I come," He wasn't implying that we're supposed to be sitting by the dock of the bay, waiting on time to roll away. *Occupy* is a military term meaning "to advance and hold, advance and hold"—to take one city, then go to another city and take that city. God wants the kingdom of God to be spread throughout the whole earth. God has chosen His people to bring heaven to earth, and His favor is upon us.

People will see what heaven is like by looking at our lives—by seeing how we walk, how we talk, how we act, how we think.

Deuteronomy 29:29 NKJV says:

> *The secret things belong to the Lord our God, but those things which are revealed belong to us and to our children forever, that we may do all the words of this law.*

When we have a revelation of the secrets of the kingdom and live according to that revelation, the world will see the difference in our lives. We will become witnesses of the gospel of the kingdom, and we will take back this earth.

I don't know about you, but I'm tired of turning on the television and seeing some mess that I can't afford to let my eyes look at. That mess exists because the kingdom of God has not been preached. However, this is a new day. God is raising up an army that will not tolerate Satan taking over this earth.

TAKING OVER THE MEDIA

Once I ministered on a major television network, and during the program I prayed for the sick. After the program aired, I met a woman who was visiting her friend in the hospital. This woman shared her testimony with me, saying, "My foot got hurt, and I couldn't walk on it. I watched the program, and you said you were going to pray for the sick. You said, 'Put your hand on the part of your body that is hurt, and God's going to heal it.' I put my hand on my foot, and you prayed, and boom! Something hit my foot. Some heat came in it, and I could walk on it just like I was whole."

"I went ahead to the doctor the next day because I had a doctor's appointment, and he said, 'There's nothing I can do for this thing. It's healed.' That changed my life!"

Unfortunately, the television station didn't respond as positively as she had. Once I prayed for the sick on that station, they called me and said, "Don't you ever do that again."

The problem wasn't the people who ran the television station. It was that Satan thinks this earth belongs to him. Enough is enough! We need to take the media, because the devil is using disobedient, deceived people to run most of the networks. Yes, some saints are in the media, but we need to take over. We're not going to take it naturally. Our problem is not people but the demonic spirits who manipulate and influence them. Only the Church can do something about them.

> *For we wrestle not against flesh and blood, but against principalities, against powers, against the rulers of the darkness of this world, against spiritual wickedness in high places. Wherefore take unto you the whole armour of God, that ye may be able to withstand in the evil day, and having done all, to stand.*
>
> EPHESIANS 6:12–13

It's called spiritual warfare. We're about to see the Church put on their military garb. We've been trying to hide who we are, but now we're going to have to come out with God's full armor on and stand against evil. We've been quiet too long, depending on the world's system and allowing the enemy to run away with what God ordained was His.

Jesus isn't coming back until His enemy is made His footstool, so we may as well come out of the closet and put our armor on.

DON'T BE TALKED OUT OF THE KINGDOM

God isn't holding the kingdom back from us. The devil is talking us out of it. If the devil says, "You can't have a happy marriage; you've been married five times," tell him, "Do you remember the woman at the well?" If he says, "You can't be in that profession; you're the wrong color," tell him, "It says according to your faith, not according to your race."

Not only will he speak to our minds, the devil will use people to make us think we don't have what it takes to receive what God gives. He'll do whatever it takes to tell us that we're not acceptable—our feet are too big, our nose is too big, our hair is too nappy, and so forth. He tries to bring condemnation on us so we can't access what we need from the kingdom. He wants to keep us broke, sick, and poor.

All we need is God's grace, which is His supernatural ability to do what we cannot do ourselves. With God's grace and the power of His kingdom, people will come out of prison and out of drug addictions to command growing businesses. God can do with a person what no human could think or imagine.

No one understood the grace of God more than David. He knew that God could work through anyone willing to receive Him and obey His Word.

When God sent the prophet Samuel to the house of Jesse to anoint the new king of Israel, David—the youngest son—was out in the field keeping the sheep. The other brothers got busy parading their biceps and triceps before Samuel, and when Samuel saw the oldest son, Eliab, he thought for sure that he was looking at the next king. He was wrong.

> *But the Lord said unto Samuel, Look not on his countenance, or on the height of his stature; because I have refused him: for the Lord seeth not as man seeth; for man looketh on the outward appearance, but the Lord looketh on the heart.*
>
> 1 SAMUEL 16:7

Samuel got the same answer from the Lord for each of the other brothers. Finally he said to Jesse, "None of these is the one. Do you have any more?"

Their father said, "Well, there's one out there keeping sheep, playing the guitar."

Samuel said, "Well, bring him in here."

The Bible says in 1 Samuel 13:14 that David was a man after God's own heart. David's heart panted for God (Ps. 42:1). When we operate in God's grace instead of our own strength, when our hearts are completely focused on God, then we will not allow the devil to talk us out of the kingdom.

GOD LOOKS ON THE HEART

No matter how many times we come into church, God sees our hearts. He sees whether we really intend to follow Him or to follow the world. God chose us because He knew our hearts. We did not have everything together, but He chose us. He didn't choose us based on how we looked on the outside. He didn't look on the way we were acting, even if we were trying to act right, but He looked on our hearts and saw that our deepest desire was to know Him. He could see in the beginning where we were going in the end.

People will check out our credentials. "Oh, you've been to Stanford. That's wonderful." We may spend a lot of money making ourselves presentable in the flesh—in that picture and on that résumé—but it's all a show. God will look straight through that flesh. He'll look clean through every grievous thing we've ever done and say, "This is the one." He sees our motives. He knows if we just want to "be somebody," or make some money and run away from Him. Our hearts tell on us.

Jesus said that everything in life has to do with the heart. In the kingdom of God, the Word of God is how God's will is accomplished in the natural realm; and the heart is where the Word of God is planted. The parable of the sower illustrates this.

Behold, there went out a sower to sow:

And it came to pass, as he sowed, some fell by the way side, and the fowls of the air came and devoured it up. And some fell on stony ground, where it had not much earth; and immediately it sprang up, because it had no depth of earth:

But when the sun was up, it was scorched; and because it had no root, it withered away.

And some fell among thorns, and the thorns grew up, and choked it, and it yielded no fruit.

And other fell on good ground, and did yield fruit that sprang up and increased; and brought forth, some thirty, and some sixty, and some an hundred.

And he said unto them, He that hath ears to hear, let him hear.

MARK 4:3-9

Here is Jesus' explanation of the parable of the sower.

The sower soweth the word.

And these are they by the way side, where the word is sown; but when they have heard, Satan cometh immediately, and taketh away the word that was sown in their hearts.

And these are they likewise which are sown on stony ground; who, when they have heard the word, immediately receive it with gladness;

And have no root in themselves, and so endure but for a time: afterward, when affliction or persecution ariseth for the word's sake, immediately they are offended.

And these are they which are sown among thorns; such as hear the word, And the cares of this world, and the deceitfulness of riches, and the lusts of other things entering in, choke the word, and it becometh unfruitful.

And these are they which are sown on good ground; such as hear the word, and receive it, and bring forth fruit, some thirtyfold, some sixty, and some an hundred.

MARK 4:14-20

Jesus tells us that the Word is the way we prosper, if our heart soil is right. If our hearts are far from desiring or knowing God, the enemy will quickly steal the Word from us. In this case our hearts are too hardened to receive the Word at all.

If our hearts are filled with stones when the Word is planted there, the roots won't be able to grow deep enough to hold us when difficult times come. So we will go back to our old way of life. We tried to get it right quickly, but we didn't remain in the revelation of the kingdom when the enemy came to challenge the Word we had received. As a result, the Word dried up and bore no fruit in our lives.

When the Word is planted in our hearts, and our hearts are filled with thorns, the thorns choke the Word. We didn't take time to weed out the evil influences of the world, and because we allowed these things to grow freely in our hearts, it was easy for them to overtake and nullify the Word we received. We want to be good ground, where our hearts are continuously seeking the Lord and free from stones and thorns. Then the Word that is planted in our hearts will bear great fruit in our lives. God knows who we are and where we are. We may not even know, but God knows. He sees directly into our hearts, and He knows when we're ready for more responsibility in the kingdom. We must remember that He is the One who promotes us.

We've got to make sure we're not promoting ourselves so that we don't get ahead of Him. God has a plan for our lives and anoints us to do His will in His timing. If we get out in front of the appointed and anointed time, we're in danger because His anointing protects us. Without it, we end up in a big struggle. That's not the way God wants us to operate.

If we find ourselves in a mess or in a ditch because our hearts have not been right and we got out of His timing and will, all we have to do is return to God and say, "God, I've been acting like a fool, and I repent and ask You now to help me." Then, with our hearts right, God will get us back on His path.

Only when our hearts are right can we live in the kingdom. Jesus said the Pharisees were blind leaders of the blind. They had all that religious education, yet most of them didn't recognize Jesus as the Messiah. A person can have all kinds of theology degrees, but that doesn't qualify them to live in kingdom reality. We can't get there except through faith in our hearts.

In order to walk in the kingdom reality, we will have to learn to let our hearts override the flesh. Peter learned this when he saw Jesus walking on the water. He said, "Lord, if that's You, bid me to come to You on the water."

Jesus said, "Come."

Peter said, "All right," and got down out of that boat.

You can imagine the rest of the disciples in the boat, and even Peter, saying, "Get back in here. Where you going? Don't be a fool." (See Matthew 14:25-29.)

The Bible says, "The flesh lusteth against the spirit" (Gal. 5:17). The flesh doesn't want to let us out, so we've got to break out. We have amazing potential inside. The flesh tries to shrink us down to the size of our minds, so we're going to have to renew our minds. God says we're His ambassadors filled with His Spirit and His kingdom. Let God be true and every man—and our flesh—a liar, because this is who we are.

REVELATION OF OUR IDENTITY

The reason many of us have not received the promises of the kingdom has never been a lack of supply. It's been a lack of revelation of who we are and what our mission is in this earth. We're not just passing through here, trying to make heaven our home. Heaven is already our home. Heaven is in us.

This kingdom of God is a new reality. Everything about it is on a higher plane: understanding, wisdom, knowledge, revelation, victory, and joy. Everything in the kingdom of God is on a spiritual plane, not a natural plane. You see, we're not natural people having a spiritual experience. We are spirits having a natural experience.

When God speaks to us about doing something, He is speaking to our spirits. He's not looking at the potential of our flesh. He speaks to us as though we're already at the level where He created us to be. In Judges 6:12, He told Gideon, "Hello there, My mighty man of valor."

Gideon heard Him, turned around, and said, "Who are you talking to?" (v. 13). He didn't have the revelation yet, but when he did he led an army into victory.

God says to you, "Hello there, my A student." "Hello there, my millionaire." He is declaring who you are in Him. If somebody calls you some nasty, dirty name, you don't even need to answer. They aren't talking to the real you, and they don't represent themselves when they say it. They are being influenced by the god of this world's system, who has blinded them from the truth.

We must get a revelation of who we are in Christ Jesus. Then we will know how we are to operate in the kingdom of God and have the confidence and faith to do what God has called us to do.

AUTHORITY OVER DEMONIC INFLUENCE

Jesus frequently met people whose actions were influenced by demonic spirits. Luke 9:51-56 recounts one of those times.

And it came to pass, when the time was come that he should be received up, he stedfastly set his face to go to Jerusalem, and sent messengers before his face: and they went, and entered into a village of the Samaritans, to make ready for him. And they did not receive him, because his face was as though he would go to Jerusalem. And when his disciples James and John saw this, they said, Lord, wilt thou that we command fire to come down from heaven, and consume them, even as Elias did? But he turned, and rebuked them, and said, Ye know not what manner of spirit ye are of. For the Son of man is not come to destroy men's lives, but to save them. And they went to another village.

The people didn't receive Jesus. They just didn't get it. They didn't realize that the answer to all their prayers was standing right in front of them. Their eyes were blinded by the devil's deception. However, Jesus did not respond by wielding physical weapons.

Matthew 26 tells of the moment when Jesus was betrayed by Judas and delivered to the Roman guards. It was a time when physical weapons seemed necessary, and Peter pulled out his sword to defend Jesus. However, Jesus saw things differently.

Then said Jesus unto him, Put up again thy sword into his place: for all they that take the sword shall perish

*with the sword. Thinkest thou that I cannot now pray
to my Father, and he shall presently give me more than
twelve legions of angels?*

MATTHEW 26:52–53

That Scripture is for us. Nothing is going to hurt us. It doesn't matter who we are in the natural world. If we're in the kingdom of God, we have access to every kingdom provision. The kingdom of God rules over every other kingdom of this world, and God can undo anything that the devil has done in our lives.

Jesus came to reverse everything that the devil has done. He came not only to cast out devils and heal the sick, but to restore people no matter where their lives had been broken. He came to put people back in the place where they belonged.

Matthew 4:23-24 says,

*And Jesus went about all Galilee, teaching in their syn-
agogues, and preaching the gospel of the kingdom, and
healing all manner of sickness and all manner of disease among the people. And his fame went throughout all
Syria: and they brought unto him all sick people that were
taken with divers diseases and torments, and those which
were possessed with devils, and those which were luna-
tick, and those that had the palsy; and he healed them.*

Jesus went through town after town and healed everyone. Therefore, when He left town, there was not one sick. Every disease and sickness is a curse, a work of the devil, and 1 John 3:8 says, "For this purpose the Son of God was manifested, that he might destroy the works of the devil." In *The Amplified Bible,* it says He came "to undo (destroy, loosen, and dissolve) the works the devil [has done]."

The devil's power is undone, destroyed, loosened, and dissolved. Isaiah 14:11-14 says this about him:

> *Thy pomp is brought down to the grave, and the noise of thy viols: the worm is spread under thee, and the worms cover thee. How art thou fallen from heaven, O Lucifer, son of the morning! how art thou cut down to the ground, which didst weaken the nations! For thou hast said in thine heart, I will ascend into heaven, I will exalt my throne above the stars of God: I will sit also upon the mount of the congregation, in the sides of the north: I will ascend above the heights of the clouds; I will be like the most High.*

Look at all those "I's." Lucifer tried to exalt himself above God, even though God had created him. He was a finite being, extremely limited compared to God. The created tried to outshine his Creator.

Verses 15-17 say,

> *Yet thou shalt be brought down to hell, to the sides of the pit. They that see thee shall narrowly look upon thee, and consider thee, saying, Is this the man that made the earth to tremble, that did shake kingdoms; That made the world as a wilderness, and destroyed the cities thereof.*

If you go to the broken-down neighborhoods, people tend to blame the brokenness on "the people." However, the devil is the one behind the destruction. His influence has blinded them into believing lies about God, Jesus, and themselves. Therefore, they serve Satan and themselves, sometimes without knowing it, making themselves and everyone around them more and more miserable.

God Is Restoring the Earth

Though the devil has corrupted and destroyed the earth, a new day is coming. Ezekiel prophesied,

> *Thus saith the Lord God; In the day that I shall have cleansed you from all your iniquities I will also cause you to dwell in the cities, and the wastes shall be builded. And the desolate land shall be tilled, whereas it lay desolate in the sight of all that passed by. And they shall say, This land that was desolate is become like the garden of Eden; and the waste and desolate and ruined cities are become fenced, and are inhabited. Then the heathen that are left round about you shall know that I the Lord build the ruined places, and plant that that was desolate: I the Lord have spoken it, and I will do it.*
>
> Ezekiel 36:33-36

When we look around our cities and see the most devastated places, we have to remember that God has a plan. His plan is to loosen and undo and destroy every bit of evidence that the devil has ever entered that neighborhood.

Our goal as God's ambassadors should be to empower people to take control over their own destinies. We can rebuild the neighborhoods by first rebuilding the people. We can deliver the Word of God to people, and then they can build up their families and neighborhoods. God hasn't given up on even the worst neighborhoods. Just watch! He's about to make them look better than we've ever seen them in our lives. He said it, and He's going to bring it to pass.

A lot of people in those neighborhoods have been fighting for their mere existence, but God's about to do a new thing. He's about to show that He is God. He doesn't need someone to have a Harvard degree to put that person on top. He can take somebody who has no degree and place them in a position of leadership over people who have many degrees.

God is going to restore. Where there is low self-esteem, He will restore confidence. Where there were thoughts of worthlessness, He will restore purpose and value.

God is about to move. Every time Jesus went through a city, He destroyed all the evidence that Satan had ever come through town. We're going to ride through the old broken neighborhoods and say, "My Lord, this looks like the Garden of Eden!"

The kingdom in operation carries the power to do a work of this magnitude and scale. The power of the kingdom is not just for healing our bodies. It's for healing the land. It's for taking a nation, a people, a culture, and a neighborhood that have been counted out and turning them around so that there is no trace that they were ever broken. We're talking about the system by which God can work and bring forth and manifest heaven upon the earth.

KNOWLEDGE TO BRING HEAVEN TO EARTH

God said, "My people are destroyed for lack of knowledge" (Hos. 4:6). We are God's people. We have the kingdom in us, but we can still be destroyed if we don't have knowledge of the kingdom. We need revelation in order to bring heaven to earth.

The kingdom of God is a spiritual operation that overtakes the natural system, which is the kingdom of darkness. The kingdom of darkness is established on fear and deception. Satan is just a bully who scares people with his words. He's like the guy in the schoolyard listing people he'll whip.

With a revelation of the kingdom, we will be the ones who say, "Hey, I heard you've got all the names of all the people that you can whip. Well, you can't whip me."

Then he'll say, "Well, I'll take it off then," and he'll take our names right off that list.

We have to challenge the devil with the Word of God, the name of Jesus, and the knowledge of the kingdom—no matter what we're facing. Under the pressures of this world's system, we may be struggling with rent or car notes. However, with the knowledge of the kingdom, we can get the struggle out of our lives. When we operate in God's system, there is more than enough for us. The kingdom has enough to take away the struggle. The kingdom allows us to live as though we were already in heaven.

In the Old Testament God established the Year of Jubilee. Every seventh year, every debt was forgiven. Through Jesus Christ, we live in a continuous Year of Jubilee. Jesus is our Year of Jubilee because all our sins are forgiven—past, present, and future. The world's system that we're living in right now, however, is not of God. It was authored by Satan, and through deception he has kept us in bondage to it. It is time for us to break free and live in Jubilee.

If we will walk in the spirit, we can dominate everything that the enemy has done to hold us in bondage. We can call things that be not as though they were. We can say everything that God says. We don't have to straddle the fence or struggle anymore. If we will let God be God in us, and if we will learn the principles of His kingdom, we will be a witness of God's goodness to the earth.

CHAPTER 11

DRAWING PEOPLE TO GOD BY MANIFESTING HIS GOODNESS

The world is waiting on a manifestation of the sons and daughters of God (Rom. 8:19). They're waiting to see what God is really like because, through darkness, they have been deceived, used, and abused. They have heard, for example, that God hates them or that God killed their kids. Unless we bring the truth and let people see how God is, many people will not come to Him.

As we walk with God and learn more about His ways, we learn who He is so that we can share His goodness with the world. As we grow in God, the things that are unseen become more real and we learn to live in the kingdom. Galatians 4:1 says,

Now I say, That the heir, as long as he is a child, differeth nothing from a servant, though he be lord of all.

In other words, "The heir, as long as he [acts childish], differeth nothing from a servant." God has given us the entire kingdom, but unless we grow up in Him we will still be slaves to the world's system. As long as we act childish and operate from our flesh rather than our spirits, we will be slaves, though we be heirs of the entire kingdom.

Everything is in the kingdom of God: healing, deliverance, prosperity, and all that we need. However, we cannot receive it with the five senses. First Corinthians 15:50 says, "Now this I say, brethren, that flesh and blood cannot inherit the kingdom of God; neither doth corruption inherit incorruption." God has designed the kingdom so that we must inherit it by the spirit.

The entire kingdom belongs to us, but we can't receive it by flesh and blood. As the Church, we have been operating at a level far beneath our means because we have resorted to the flesh. This has been a problem in the Church since the days of Paul, who wrote in 1 Corinthians 3:1-3:

> *And I, brethren, could not speak unto you as unto spiritual, but as unto carnal, even as unto babes in Christ. I have fed you with milk, and not with meat: for hitherto ye were not able to bear it, neither yet now are ye able. For ye are yet carnal: for whereas there is among you envying, and strife, and divisions, are ye not carnal, and walk as men?*

The Amplified Bible says, "Are you not unspiritual and of the flesh, behaving yourselves after a human standard and like mere (unchanged) men?"

In this kingdom, we are not mere anything. Faith links us to the supernatural Creator, and we now have "super" attached to us. We are super, and there is some super on our natural. We have supernatural abilities because we are in Christ Jesus, our supernatural Creator.

FREE TO OPERATE IN A HIGHER REALITY

The reality that we're walking in from day to day is a physical reality, but God does not want us to be bound by that reality. He wants to set us free to operate in His higher reality, a reality that functions beyond space and time, and which is more real than what we perceive with our natural senses.

The kingdom of God is a reality in the unseen dimension that is more real than what we can see. In fact, it created the sensory dimension that we live in. Genesis says that in the beginning, God created the heaven and the earth. God is the Creator, Elohim. He is Jehovah, the self-existing One. He doesn't need to go to anybody else; He is the source.

When God says He can bless us, He can bless us by Himself. He doesn't need anything around us. He can bless us in the middle of the desert. He can bless us on the top of a desolate mountain. He can bless us in the middle of a violent situation in the neighborhood. He can bless us in the middle of the worst economy there is. We can be blessed in abundance because our provisions are from God, not from the natural world around us.

In Genesis 1:9, God says, "Let the dry land appear." Immediately dry land began to appear. Whatever God said, He saw. We know land is matter, and the Bible says in John 4:24

that God is a spirit. The One who is a spirit created all physical matter. The greater reality is not the matter but the Spirit.

When God looked at the earth and saw a formless and dark void, He didn't say, "Whoo! Isn't it dark out there?" Rather, He spoke what He wanted. He was not moved by the reality of the physical realm. God doesn't want us to get anxious and upset about what we see because He created us just like Him. He created us to be able to speak what we need into existence.

WITNESSES OF THE KINGDOM REALITY

God wants us to live from the kingdom reality as His witnesses, who will change and rearrange this world. He's enabled us to speak to storms and have them obey us. God wants people to see what heaven is like. He wants them to witness what He is like, and we are His witnesses. Jesus told us to pray, "Thy kingdom come, Thy will be done in earth, as it is in heaven" (Matt. 6:10).

The will of God can't be done unless the kingdom of God comes, and it has come inside of us. Now God wants us to demonstrate to people what heaven is really like.

Romans 2:4 says,

> *Or despisest thou the riches of his goodness and forbearance and longsuffering; not knowing that the goodness of God leadeth thee to repentance?*

The goodness of God is what will lead the people of the world to repentance.

When our church was new, we met in a storefront building in a really rough area of Chicago. We had to clean up whiskey bottles before we could have service. We had to leave the door open because it was so hot in that little room. People packed in there, but they didn't come there in droves.

However, when we moved up to Madison Street, we were in a better environment and the place looked nice. All of a sudden, people started coming in great numbers. We went to three services, and people lined up down the sidewalk waiting for the next service—as if we were giving away hamburgers in there!

Then, when we moved to the mall, we were getting more souls saved than ever before. We drew more people in as we moved into nicer facilities, and that's because people look on the outside.

> *Man looketh on the outward appearance, but the Lord looketh on the heart.*
> 1 SAMUEL 16:7

People want to see on the outside what we have on the inside. This is why we are God's witnesses. In His name we're praying for the sick and they're being healed. In His name we're casting out devils and people are being set free from oppression. In His name we're able to provide a car for the single mom of four down the street who needs to get to work.

In order to operate in this kingdom reality and share it with the world, however, we have to grow up. If we remain childish in the spirit, we are nothing but slaves to the world, though we are recipients of the entire kingdom. We've got all this capacity but act like babies. To impact the world for God's kingdom, we're going to have to grow up in faith and move in the power of God.

TIME FOR A DEMONSTRATION

God put us in this world as His witnesses to demonstrate His power and goodness to all people. Matthew 24:14 says, "This gospel of the kingdom shall be preached in all the world for a witness unto all nations; and then shall the end come."

We're going to demonstrate the gospel of the kingdom of God, and we do that just like we do everything else: by faith. Faith is the link to the supernatural, and faith creates the plan God has for this natural world. We know from Romans 10:17 that faith comes by hearing the Word of God, and in the last couple of decades, the Church has been bombarded with teaching the Word of God.

God never intended for this much Word to go forth without demonstration of His power and goodness. We don't need one more sermon before we can demonstrate the kingdom because we have the kingdom in us. We can take what we've got and demonstrate the kingdom of God on the earth right now.

For too long we've believed that what the world says is true, but what is true is what God said. If He didn't say it, then it isn't true. What He said about us is true. Maybe people have called us names, but if it's not what God has called us then it's not true. And He says that the kingdom of God is in us, that we are His witnesses, all authority has been given to us, and we can demonstrate His power and goodness to those around us.

The deceiver draws people into the flesh, but if we focus on the things of God, our bodies will demonstrate the light of God. We'll be full of revelation knowledge. We'll walk in such a way that the wicked one cannot touch us. We'll love people when they can't stand us. We'll speak well of people when they've been running us down.

DIRECTIONS FOR LIFE

Satan is a deceiver, and if we only approach life from our five senses we will easily be deceived. However, if we focus on the Scriptures, we will receive the knowledge we need to operate in a realm above the flesh. We will no longer wander through life blindly, but we will receive our directions from the Spirit of God to our spirit.

If we try to demonstrate the kingdom without God's Word and the leading of the Holy Spirit, however, we can get into trouble quickly. A good example of this in the natural was when I decided to get in good physical shape. After working out for a couple days, I could hardly walk. My personal trainer looked at how I was doing my exercises and said, "That's all wrong." No wonder I was so sore! I needed his guidance into knowledge about exercising.

When we spend time in the Scriptures, the Holy Spirit is imparting knowledge about functioning in the kingdom. We've got to quiet our mind and say, "Hey, wait a minute. I've been trying this for twenty years, and I'm still hurting." It's time to talk to our Personal Trainer. It's time to get some knowledge and guidance from Him, then we will start seeing some results—without near as much pain.

We're transitioning out of the flesh and into the spirit, learning how to live according to God's kingdom, so we need some direction from the Holy Spirit and the Word of God. Whether we need healing or material provision, as we pursue knowledge of the Scriptures we'll see the manifestation of the kingdom in our lives. The enemy wants to keep us from that knowledge, but as we spend time in the Word that knowledge will just keep growing.

This is the way that we've got to live. Habakkuk 2:4 says, "The just shall live by his faith." Faith is not something that we use like a spare tire when we get in trouble. It's a way that we have to live all day, every day. We have to live in this new kingdom reality in order to experience it and become witnesses of it.

THE LAW OF ABUNDANCE

Jesus came preaching John 10:10. In 3 John 2 it says, "Beloved, I wish above all things that thou mayest prosper and be in health, even as thy soul prospereth." If you see yourself running out, your soul has not prospered. By the soul I mean the mind, will, emotions, intellect, and imagination. God's promise to us, His children, is "they shall not be ashamed in the evil time (when times are hard): and in the days of famine they shall be satisfied (have abundance)" (Ps. 37:19).

One of the greatest witnesses of God's kingdom is His provision. When we spend time in God's presence, we will find that He is a God of abundant provision. He has already laid up an inexhaustible supply for His people. Psalm 91:1 says, "He that dwelleth in the secret place of the most High shall abide under the shadow of the Almighty." The Almighty is El Shaddai, God all sufficient, all bountiful. The God who sees and provides.

As I mentioned in an earlier chapter, I first learned some of these truths years ago when I was working as a sales manager for a large international computer company. The economy was down and computer sales were scarcely happening. The other managers in my branch office, along with myself, would go to lunch and have a pity party including me, We were coming up on the end of the month which is the time our boss expected us to report our sales. Things were so bad we barely had anything to report.

Approaching the last day of the month, I began to feel convicted about using my faith. I came in early on that last day and received a call from my sister who asked me, "How's it going?" Without thinking I said, "It's going great, and if you call back at five o'clock, I'll have more business to put on the books than we can handle." This was purely my faith speaking because my head or intellect never would have said that, not with such a short timetable and the economy being that bad.

Well, about midday my salespeople began to call in, each one informing me of unexpected, large computer orders. God was moving. By the end of the day, I had so much business we couldn't book it all. My boss told me, "Save some of this until next month." Doesn't this sound a little like Peter's catch of fish that ran his boat over? You see, God's Word never changes. What it did for Peter, it will do for me and it will do for you. This is the kingdom of God at work through us. No matter what the environmental circumstances, we will have plenty.

Notice also, what normally takes days, weeks, or even years in the kingdom only takes hours, minutes, or even seconds. In the kingdom of God you are operating in the realm of God, and in the realm of God there is no time. In the Spirit, time ceases to exist and we can use our faith to override time. Faith can slow time down, speed time up, or even bring time to a screeching halt. This is real time management and the power of the kingdom within.

When we're bound by the world's system, that is, time and matter become the boundary by which we define reality, we think we're in shortage. We never have enough. However, that's a deception that the enemy has used to try to keep people bound and in scarcity. If we're afraid of running out, we're not thinking right. We're thinking very negatively, like the unbeliever. But if our minds have been bathed in the law of abundance that we understand from God's Word, we think right. People can have a billion dollars and still have a poverty spirit binding them on every hand. They can be stuck in a perception where they don't have enough for themselves and don't see anybody's need but their own. We've got to wake up to that because that's what the enemy wants.

The kingdom of God is heaven on earth. It's about sharing; it's about blessing people; and preventing misfortune in their lives. It's about helping people so they don't have to go through hardship in their lives. Let's think like God thinks. If we see a person who can't pay their rent and we've got some means, let's offer some help. This demonstrates God's goodness to them and shows them His kingdom.

Some people have this mentality that if someone else has a big piece of pie, we can't get a big piece. That's not true. There is plenty for all, not only naturally but supernaturally. We don't have to be jealous or envious of anything anybody else has. That thought didn't dawn on me until I started studying abundance and meditating in the Word of God concerning it. Meditation brings revelation, which provides access to the eternal realm of

God, where all our provisions are laid up. If the physical supply is not enough, then there is more in the realm of the Spirit, the heavens. We access it by faith, which I call "currency of the kingdom," because the more faith you have, the more of your provisions you can transfer from this unseen reservoir into your natural life. One of the reasons Jesus came to earth was to reconnect heaven and earth, which had been separated by the sin of Adam. There is an invisible supply of God's kingdom!

Jesus said, "I am come that they might have life, and that they might have it more abundantly" (John 10:10). The way we receive that life is by getting past the limitations of our minds and entering the possibilities of the spirit by having faith in God's Word. We have to get God's promises on our minds and in our hearts because He is El Shaddai—He is abundance. He doesn't give a little bit. He gives enough to each of us to feed thousands. If we would let God use us, He could feed the nation of Haiti through just one person. The potential in every believer with the kingdom within is awesome.

THEY WILL KNOW US BY OUR LOVE

As ambassadors of the kingdom, we've got to touch everybody. We've got to touch the up-and-overs and the down-and-outers. We've got to touch the saints who have it and the saints who don't. If we have plenty, we've got to help those who don't. If we only have little, we've got to help those who don't have anything. This is the way the Church will be known. The world thinks differently. The world wants people to struggle, and they just love to watch them do it. They'll look right at people while they're going through a trial and won't lift a finger, even with all their resources. That's why something has to happen to the mind when we come into the kingdom of God. It has to be converted. It has to be bathed in the love of God. It has to see things as God sees them. It has to stop being quick to notice how poorly somebody's doing without wanting to do anything about it. Instead, it must always think in terms of the compassion of the Lord, finding a way to make a difference in people's lives.

We've got to listen for God's instructions as we operate as His witnesses in this earth. We cannot do it without hearing His voice, because Satan will deceive us if we are operating in the flesh. It is His truth that will make us free and help others to be set free (John 8:32).

One time God told me to buy somebody in my church a suit, and I thought I'd misheard Him. This brother dressed sharp—sharper than I did. However, Jesus said He judged no one according to appearance. He heard God and depended only on Him.

Before this man left church one day, he came up to talk with me for a little while. As he was going away, God said, "I told you to buy him a suit." So I said to one of the ushers, "Go call this man," and I told my wife, "Make out a check for this man. God said to buy him a suit." When the man came, I said, "I don't know what this is all about, but God told me to buy you a suit or something." I hated to say suit.

I gave him the check, and a few days later he called me and said, "Pastor, I want to tell you about that money you gave me yesterday. A friend of mine had gotten burned out, and God put it on my heart to bring him over to the house to pick out any suits he wanted and take them. I obeyed, and that man picked out some of my suits." Suddenly, I understood that God was replacing those suits, but if I had walked only by what I could see I wouldn't have been a part of that opportunity to share God's love and goodness in that special way.

We must listen to God's voice and then obey Him, in spite of what we see with our natural eyes or think in our natural minds.

GROWING UP TO REACH THE WORLD

In spiritual terms, to be a child is to be moved by emotions and by the things that we see. It's to fail to cooperate because we want our own way. As long as we are spiritually childish, we are no different than servants or slaves, though we are lords of all. (See Galatians 4:1.)

Tradition has emphasized a very personal spirituality. If we try to ask people about what they believe outside of the church, often they answer, "That's personal." That is the thinking that people have had in the world's system: Religion is something we don't talk about. That is unscriptural thinking, and it has caused Christians to withdraw from society instead of manifesting God's glory and being witnesses for Him.

Jesus said, "And this gospel of the kingdom shall be preached in all the world for a witness unto all nations; and then shall the end come" (Matt. 24:14). Our mandate is to take the gospel of the kingdom to the world, not only in word but in demonstration. When we demonstrate the goodness of God, His goodness draws people to repentance, which brings them into the kingdom of God.

During Jesus' ministry, He ministered on the shoreline. He ministered to business people. He ministered to the people in high authority and politics, and He ministered the principles of life to the common person. He said, "So is the kingdom of God, as if a man should cast seed into the ground; and should sleep, and rise night and day" (Mark 4:26-27). This is the way Jesus cast the seeds of the Word. He preached and demonstrated the gospel of the kingdom nonstop.

Jesus showed people how to get their needs met. He demonstrated that God was not a god of scarcity, or even a god who has just enough. God is the more-than-enough God. He is El Shaddai, the God of abundance who supplies every need. Nothing is impossible for Him. He showed people that God could take two fish and feed five thousand men plus women and children. He showed people that God could take a man who was dead four days and raise him up. He showed Peter how to catch as many fish as his boat could hold. He showed people that God, the same God who introduced Himself to Abraham, saying, "I'm going to bless you and your seed."

Jesus called the people of the earth to stop acting, strategizing, and thinking like the world and to enter into the kingdom of God. He wants us in the world but not of the world. Once we are born again, the kingdom of God comes inside of us so that we can go into the world and change it, converting others and bringing them into the kingdom. The kingdom of God enables us to live above the world's system, but it enables us to demonstrate God's goodness to the world in power. We are His witnesses. To do this, we must grow up in Him. We must not forget that there is a power available to us that can only be attained through denying ourselves and giving Him full reign in our hearts. Jesus says in Luke 9:23,

> *If any man will come after me, let him deny himself, and take up his cross daily, and follow me.*

The kingdom of God demands that we die to self and allow God to rule our lives. It requires us to allow Him to work through us so that we might attain what He ordained for us from the beginning of the world, before we were even born in this earth.

The kingdom of God has come, and it has come through us. When we grow up and operate in God's love and Word, we will demonstrate His goodness to the world. As a result, many will be drawn to Jesus, because the world is hungry for the only love that can satisfy the longing of their souls. No matter what they say or do, they want to see the manifestation of the sons and daughters of God because deep inside they know that is their only hope.

It's time for the Church to wake up, to grow up, to appropriate our inheritance, to bless and heal those around us—to show the world who God really is.

CHAPTER 12

ANGELIC ASSISTANCE

As God's sons and daughters, we are spirit beings. Therefore, we need to learn to focus on the spirit realm. One of the ways we do that is to set our attention on what is eternal instead of what is temporal. In 2 Corinthians 4:16-18, Paul makes an important contrast between the outward man and the inward man, and relates this to how we prosper in eternal reality.

> *For which cause we faint not; but though our outward man perish, yet the inward man is renewed day by day. For our light affliction, which is but for a moment, worketh for us a far more exceeding and eternal weight of glory; while we look not at the things which are seen, but at the things which are not seen: for the things which are seen are temporal; but the things which are not seen are eternal.*

If we can see it, feel it, touch it, taste it, and smell it, then it is temporal. If we keep our eyes on something that is temporal, then our affliction will be heavy and long. On the other hand, if we focus on what we can't see, the affliction or difficulties that may come into our lives are momentary and light.

We want to get through difficult situations just as quickly as possible! We don't want to always be going through hard times. In Romans, Paul tells us how to direct our focus so that we can come through those situations quickly and unscathed. Romans 4:13 in *The Amplified Bible* says,

> *For the promise to Abraham or his posterity, that he should inherit the world, did not come through [observing the commands of] the Law but through the righteousness of faith.*

Abraham inherited the earth and overcame his difficulties, not through following a list of rules, but by the righteousness that came by his faith. We have to realize that the things in the earth don't belong to the devil. They belong to us. As the righteousness of God in Christ, we are heirs, and the entire kingdom is our inheritance. Furthermore, any trial we encounter is subject to the kingdom of God.

Verse 16 in the *New Living Translation* says,

> *The promise is received by faith. It is given as a free gift. And we are all certain to receive it, whether or not we live according to the law of Moses, if we have faith like Abraham's. For Abraham is the father of all who believe.*

We are to be more than conquerors just like our spiritual father, Abraham. He met all the challenges of his life by having faith in God and His promises over any of the temporal circumstances he faced. As a result, God delivered him again and again in impossible situations.

SENT INTO THE IMPOSSIBLE

In order to access our inheritance, we will have to face some situations that are impossible for us on our own. God says, "Get ready because the giants in the land of your inheritance are stronger and mightier than you are, but I'm going to enable you to conquer them." This is what He told the Israelites before they entered Canaan, the land of promise.

> *The Lord thy God shall bring thee into the land whither thou goest to possess it, and hath cast out many nations before thee, the Hittites, and the Girgashites, and the Amorites, and the Canaanites, and the Perizzites, and the Hivites, and the Jebusites, seven nations greater and mightier than thou.*
>
> DEUTERONOMY 7:1

When we face these seemingly impossible situations, we cannot neglect the ministry of angels because they provide the help we need. We can't see the angels, but they are more real than what we can see. God prepared the Israelites for Canaan with the knowledge that His power would deliver them, and we know that the agents of that power in the spirit realm are His angels.

And when the Lord thy God shall deliver them before thee;
thou shalt smite them, and utterly destroy them; thou shalt
make no covenant with them, nor shew mercy unto them.

DEUTERONOMY 7:2

In verse 1, God said that the enemy would be greater and mightier than them, but in verse 2, He says that His people will smite them. We're going to meet some giants that are bigger and stronger than us, but God will empower us to utterly destroy them and send His angels to help us. This is not a deal where we have to work by ourselves, of ourselves, or with our own resources. Our sufficiency is of God, for God will supply everything we need to win every battle.

Again, in Deuteronomy 9:1, God sends His people into the impossible. He says,

Hear, O Israel: Thou art to pass over Jordan this day, to
go in to possess nations greater and mightier than thyself,
cities great and fenced up to heaven.

He sent them in to not only take the people but to take back some property for the kingdom of God.

God is taking each of us into the land of our inheritance. The land is occupied by the enemy, but He's giving it back into our hands. However, we have to do it His way. We have to seek first the kingdom and His righteousness—His way of doing things—and all these things will be added unto us.

TWO REPORTS: FLESH AND SPIRIT

In Numbers 13, we read about the twelve spies coming back from scouting out the land of Canaan. In verses 27-29, we see a negative report from ten of the spies.

> *And they told him, and said, We came unto the land whither thou sentest us, and surely it floweth with milk and honey; and this is the fruit of it. Nevertheless the people be strong that dwell in the land, and the cities are walled, and very great: and moreover we saw the children of Anak [giants] there. The Amalekites dwell in the land of the south: and the Hittites, and the Jebusites, and the Amorites, dwell in the mountains: and the Canaanites dwell by the sea, and by the coast of Jordan.*

Then in verse 30, we hear a good report from one of the spies.

> *And Caleb stilled the people before Moses, and said, Let us go up at once, and possess it; for we are well able to overcome it.*

However, in verse 31, the ten spies immediately interjected their fears.

> *But the men that went up with him said, We be not able to go up against the people; for they are stronger than we.*

There were two reports: the report of the flesh and the report of the spirit. In the natural and according to the flesh, it was true that the Canaanites were mightier than the Israelites. However, according to the spirit, the Canaanites could never

189

measure up to the Israelites. Unfortunately, Israel chose to believe the evil report of the ten spies, and they wandered in the wilderness for forty years as a result.

"WATCH YOUR MOUTH"

Earlier in the Scriptures, we read God's words to Moses, preparing him for what would come in the Israelites' journey.

> *Behold, I send an Angel before thee, to keep thee in the way, and to bring thee into the place which I have prepared. Beware of him, and obey his voice, provoke him not; for he will not pardon your transgressions: for my name is in him. But if thou shalt indeed obey his voice, and do all that I speak; then I will be an enemy unto thine enemies, and an adversary unto thine adversaries. For mine Angel shall go before thee, and bring thee in unto the Amorites, and the Hittites, and the Perizzites, and the Canaanites, the Hivites, and the Jebusites: and I will cut them off.*
>
> EXODUS 23:20-23

Notice, He said, "Provoke him not." In other words, He was saying, "Watch your mouth, Moses. Don't speak foolishness and make your angel mad."

When those ten spies came back and said, "We cannot take those giants; they are stronger than we are. The cities are walled in, so we can't even get in there," they were speaking an evil report because it was against God's plan for their lives. Their words of unbelief provoked the angel of the Lord and caused them to forfeit their inheritance.

When we enter impossible situations, we cannot look at what the experts say, what the professionals say, what the doctors say, what the lawyers say, or what the judge says. We have to stand on what God says: "You say what I say because I'm taking you into a place where they are too big for you. You keep your mouth right because you need the angels working with you. Where I'm taking you, the people have more education, more status, and more money than you do. I'm taking you into the land of your inheritance, and you're taking it all back if you speak words of faith."

GOD PREPARES US WITH HIS WORD

In Joshua 1:2-5, God spoke to Joshua after Moses died. With His word, He prepares Joshua for the great task of leading Israel into Canaan.

> *Moses my servant is dead; now therefore arise, go over this Jordan, thou, and all this people, unto the land which I do give to them, even to the children of Israel. Every place that the sole of your foot shall tread upon, that have I given unto you, as I said unto Moses. From the wilderness and this Lebanon even unto the great river, the river Euphrates, all the land of the Hittites, and unto the great sea toward the going down of the sun, shall be your coast. There shall not any man be able to stand before thee all the days of thy life: as I was with Moses, so I will be with thee: I will not fail thee, nor forsake thee.*

When God sends us into the land of our inheritance, He prepares us with His Word. When we listen to His Word, we focus on the invisible. Then, when we can see the invisible, we can do the impossible. We don't have anything to fear because we know we have invisible help surrounding us. God has assigned angels to us, and they are more powerful than anything we can see with our natural eyes. When we prepare to enter the land of our inheritance, we need to place our faith in God's ability to deliver us and supply us with angelic help. Angels are going to bring us into and through impossible situations. With God all things are possible. When we are with God, He is with us and He will never fail us or forsake us.

As we march toward the land of promise, we can't say what it looks like. We have to say what God said. Then God will give us things that are bigger than what we could have imagined on our own.

My wife and I experienced this when we were looking for a house in Minnesota some 20 years ago. After about three days of looking, God laid it on my heart that I was to ask my wife which house she liked. I said, "Well, Baby, the Lord told me to ask you which one you like."

She said, "No, you mean which one can we afford?"

I said, "No, He didn't tell me that. He told me to ask you which one you like." If we can believe the Bible and get our mouths right, then we can get our lives right. We are joint-heirs with Jesus Christ. He has lawfully inherited all things, and in Him so have we.

Psalm 105:43-44 says,

And he brought forth his people with joy, and his chosen with gladness: and gave them the lands of the heathen: and they inherited the labour of the people.

Proverbs 13:22 says,

A good man leaveth an inheritance to his children's children: and the wealth of the sinner is laid up for the just.

Most of us look at that verse and wonder when that wealth will be "un-laid up." The question is, how long are we going to leave it laid up? God has freely given us all things. We don't need to struggle to make a living; we've inherited all things. Instead, we're working for a giving. We work to serve others better, and the inheritance becomes available to us as we work for a giving.

When I asked my wife, "Which house do you like?" she said, "Well, I like that big white one up on the hill with that circular driveway." We had about five hundred dollars in savings at that time. However, we weren't looking at what we had; we were looking at what He had. My wife wanted the biggest house we looked at, and we had nothing!

I said, "Let's pray," and we got down on our knees and started praying. God spoke to me and said, "Get up and go over there and point at that house." As soon as I told my wife, she said, "Let's go." She is a faith woman, and we had come this far by faith.

We got up, went over to the house, and pointed at that house. I said, "House, I'm talking to you. In the name of Jesus Christ of Nazareth, sell to us." I put my hand back on the steering wheel and drove off. The deal was done. Now the angels began their work. I had obeyed the voice of the Lord.

We shouldn't look at something we can afford when we can get something we can't afford and get it debt-free. "According to your faith be it unto you" (Matt. 9:29). We're obeying God and placing all of our faith in Him, and God wants to show people that He is bigger than their god.

We started believing God for a twenty-thousand-dollar down payment. My boss at the computer company called me in and said, "Hey, Bill. We've got a contest for managers."

I said, "Hey, that's great. What's the contest?" He said, "Well, it's five thousand dollars." I said, "Is that right?"

He said, "Yeah. I have good news for you. You won."

That's just one example of how that twenty-thousand-dollar down payment came in because I spoke what God told me to speak instead of my doubts and natural reasoning. The whole situation was completely supernatural. We set something in motion in the spirit realm with faith in God's promise and with our words. By sowing a sizeable seed, we purchased our next house with cash and it was brand new.

WE'VE GOT TO SPEAK

When Jesus came into the room where Jairus's daughter lay dead, He said, "She's not dead; she's just asleep." (See Mark 5:39.) He wasn't trying to impress people. By His words, He was getting the supernatural to move on His behalf.

It's a law that we've got to speak. God can't go past our conversation. Angels are assigned to bring us into the impossible, but they're waiting on the voice of faith. Psalm 103:20 says that the angels hearken to the voice of the Lord, and we are that voice!

If we know we've got some big angels standing behind us waiting for someone to try to lay a hand on us, we'll stand tall for our God. When I was a little boy, I got in a fight with a bigger boy. He was threatening me until my big brother came around the corner. As soon as he looked at my brother, I saw him change. I wondered what happened. Then I saw my brother, and I started gaining confidence. I said, "Now why did you hit me?" My attitude and my words changed because I knew I had some help.

When Nebuchadnezzar tried to get Shadrach, Meshach, and Abednego to bow down to his system, the Hebrew men spoke words that activated their angels. Their story teaches us that when laws are made against our God, we don't have to bow because we have angelic assistance.

When King Nebuchadnezzar found out that the boys were planning not to bow to his idol, he was very angry and said,

> *If ye worship not, ye shall be cast the same hour into the midst of a burning fiery furnace; and who is that God that shall deliver you out of my hands?*
>
> DANIEL 3:15

Despite the king's rage, these giants of faith—Shadrach, Meschach, and Abednego—answered and said to the king, "O Nebuchadnezzar, we are not careful to answer thee in this matter" (v. 16). In other words, they were saying, "We're not worried what will happen to us if we answer the right way."

Then they continued,

> *If it be so, our God whom we serve is able to deliver us from the burning fiery furnace, and he will deliver us out of thine hand, O king.*
>
> DANIEL 3:17

We've got to watch our mouths, as these three men did. When it gets tight, we need to get right. We need to say what God said because we have help. The angels are standing there waiting on our words. It might look impossible, but God is the God of the impossible. There is nothing too hard for Him. He will deliver us. He didn't say He might; He said that He will.

So many Christian people bow down because they don't know they have help. If they realized the supernatural power that stood behind their words of faith, they would change their world. Those three Hebrew boys were thrown into the fire, and in verses 24-26 we see a changed King Nebuchadnezzar.

Then Nebuchadnezzar the king was astonished, and rose up in haste, and spake, and said unto his counsellors, Did not we cast three men bound into the midst of the fire? They answered and said unto the king, True, O king. He answered and said, Lo, I see four men loose, walking in the midst of the fire, and they have no hurt; and the form of the fourth is like the Son of God.

Then Nebuchadnezzar came near to the mouth of the burning fiery furnace, and spake, and said, Shadrach, Meshach, and Abednego, ye servants of the most high God, come forth, and come hither. Then Shadrach, Meshach, and Abednego, came forth of the midst of the fire.

Shadrach, Meshach, and Abednego were loosed from those bindings. They became a witness to all nations, and they were promoted. When we watch our words in the midst of the impossible, angels come to deliver us, promote us, and make us witnesses to the nations.

ANGELIC ARMIES

In 2 Kings 6, we find Elisha surrounded by the Syrian army because they found out that he was telling Israel how the Syrians were going to attack. When the king of Syria found out that the prophet was revealing his secrets, he sent a host of Syrians after this one man. Verse 15 says,

> *And when the servant of the man of God was risen early, and gone forth, behold, an host compassed the city both with horses and chariots. And his servant said unto him, Alas, my master! how shall we do?*

Elisha's servant absolutely panicked because he thought that there was no escape for them. Hebrews 2:3 says, "How shall we escape, if we neglect so great salvation." If we neglect the provisions of our salvation, including the ministry of angels, we cannot escape impossible situations. However, with faith in God's Word and the ministry of angels, we can overcome every obstacle.

Verse 16 shows us Elisha's response. "Fear not: for they that be with us are more than they that be with them." Fear will paralyze our movement forward. It will stop our angels, and it will keep us from our deliverance. Whatever the case may be, we just have to shake off fear. We have to bind the spirit of fear and cast it out. No matter what happens, no matter what we feel in our bodies, we *fear not.*

> *And Elisha prayed, and said, Lord, I pray thee, open his eyes, that he may see. And the Lord opened the eyes of the*

young man; and he saw: and, behold, the mountain was
full of horses and chariots of fire round about Elisha.

2 KINGS 6:17

Angels surrounded the Syrian army, and they blinded them according to Elisha's word (v. 18). God didn't send one angel for Elisha and his servant; He sent thousands of them, and one angel could slaughter 185,000 men. (See 2 Kings 19:35.) God is always a God of more than enough.

The Bible says heaven has an innumerable number of angels (Heb. 12:22). We can't even count the number of angels that God has. If He had to send every one of them on our behalf, He would do just that. We don't ever need to be afraid when we face impossible situations because He has provided an angelic army to minister to us.

> *But to which of the angels said he at any time, Sit on my*
> *right hand, until I make thine enemies thy footstool? Are*
> *they not all ministering spirits, sent forth to minister for*
> *them who shall be heirs of salvation?*

HEBREWS 1:13–14

We are the heirs of salvation, and God has commanded His angels to minister *for* us. That means He says to the angels, "Whenever they speak My Word, you do what they say."

WAR IN THE HEAVENLIES

In Daniel 10:12-13, we read about an angel speaking to Daniel:

> *Fear not, Daniel: for from the first day that thou didst set*
> *thine heart to understand, and to chasten thyself before thy*

God, thy words were heard, and I am come for thy words.
But the prince of the kingdom of Persia withstood me one
and twenty days.

Daniel's words activated the angel to move on Daniel's behalf. This illustrates that our confession has a lot to do with our possession.

The first verse of this chapter said, "In the third year of Cyrus king of Persia a thing was revealed unto Daniel." In verse 13, we read about "the prince of the kingdom of Persia." This latter prince is a spirit. The human, natural leadership of the land was being controlled by a demon prince. That is the way Satan controls things in this earth—by demonic influence over men and women.

The devil wants leaders in place who will do the most for his kingdom. The devil believes in stealing, killing, and destroying, and he wants people in governmental offices who will be puppets for him. The leaders under his control think the devil's thoughts are their own, but he's just pulling their strings.

There was a strong man controlling Hitler, and he was having Hitler kill Jews and other innocent people. If somebody hadn't stopped him, he would have taken over this earth. God raised up a nation called the United States of America, and He has always used this nation for judgment. This nation is one nation under God, and it's going to stay like that. The enemy has tried to put people in judicial seats of authority to take God out of our nation, and he has had teachers give false instruction to their students about God and life. These people don't know they're wrong because they've been taught by others who are under the influence of the devil. But our nation has lots of Daniels who know how to pray God's will to be done on earth as it is in heaven, and we the church are beginning to challenge the enemy's strongholds in the United States.

It's time for the Church to take back what the enemy has stolen. The devil hasn't put up anything that God can't pull down. All of us have been deceived at some point in our lives, but we're saved now. There is hope for every one of those leaders whom the devil has tried to use to promote his kingdom. They need Jesus, and we are here to be witnesses to them of His kingdom.

In verse 13, we read how the angel was able to break through the devil's ranks to come to Daniel's side.

Lo, Michael, one of the chief princes, came to help me.

Michael is one of the chief princes of the angels, and he loves a fight. He is skilled in breaking through the devil's defenses and making the devil and his demons bow down. There is a war being waged in the heavenlies. The devil wants to keep us from our inheritance so that he can keep the world in darkness. However, when we keep our confession right and stand in faith, God will always get our inheritance through to us and make us witnesses to the nations. He has enough angels, and they know how to fight. The devil can't hold anything back from us.

The earth is the Lord's and the fullness thereof, and He has given us dominion over it. We are joined with Him in Jesus Christ, who has legally inherited all things. He will send His angels to bring us through impossible situations to make us witnesses of God's goodness to the entire world. When we focus on the unseen, when we live from the spirit and in faith and total dependence on God, we will conquer impossible situations and inherit the earth, and we will be conduits for God's miraculous power.

CHAPTER 13

TIME FOR MIRACLES

First Corinthians 4:20 says, "For the kingdom of God is not in word, but in *power*." In other words, the kingdom of God is in demonstration. God never intended for so much Word to go forth without a demonstration. The demonstration part confirms the Word that is preached. That's how Jesus added multitudes at a time to His followers, and we're a continuation of Jesus' ministry. God is saying today, "It is time for miracles."

First Corinthians 2:4-5 says,

And my speech and my preaching was not with enticing words of man's wisdom, but in demonstration of the Spirit and of power: that your faith should not stand in the wisdom of men, but in the power of God.

Paul didn't rely on his own wisdom or ability to speak of the Scriptures, but he relied on God's demonstration of the Scriptures to convince people that his words were true.

THE FULL GOSPEL

The Word spoken under the anointing of the kingdom comes with power. Romans 15:18-19 says,

> *For I will not dare to speak of any of those things which Christ hath not wrought by me, to make the Gentiles obedient, by word and deed, through mighty signs and wonders, by the power of the Spirit of God; so that from Jerusalem, and round about unto Illyricum, I have fully preached the gospel of Christ.*

Paul is talking about the full gospel. He's talking about a demonstration of signs and wonders to confirm the Word that he has preached.

Jesus preached that kind of gospel. Matthew 4:23-24 says,

> *Jesus went about all Galilee, teaching in their synagogues, and preaching the gospel of the kingdom, and healing all manner of sickness and all manner of disease among the people. And his fame went throughout all Syria: and they brought unto him all sick people that were taken with divers diseases and torments, and those which were possessed with devils, and those which were lunatick, and those that had the palsy; and he healed them.*

He healed everybody of everything they had. In Matthew 10, we see Jesus addressing His disciples, preparing them to continue His ministry in the earth.

> *And when he had called unto him his twelve disciples, he gave them power against unclean spirits, to cast them*

out, and to heal all manner of sickness and all manner of disease.

And as ye go, preach, saying, The kingdom of heaven is at hand. Heal the sick, cleanse the lepers, raise the dead, cast out devils: freely ye have received, freely give.

MATTHEW 10:1,7-8

Jesus' disciples include His followers today—you and me. When we are sent out as people of God, we are sent out with power to demonstrate His kingdom. The gospel of the kingdom is to be preached as a witness, as a demonstration. Mark 16:15-18 says,

And he said unto them, Go ye into all the world, and preach the gospel to every creature. He that believeth and is baptized shall be saved; but he that believeth not shall be damned. And these signs shall follow them that believe; In my name shall they cast out devils; they shall speak with new tongues; they shall take up serpents; and if they drink any deadly thing, it shall not hurt them; they shall lay hands on the sick, and they shall recover.

Verses 19-20 tell us what happened after Jesus shared these words with His disciples.

So then after the Lord had spoken unto them, he was received up into heaven, and sat on the right hand of God. And they went forth, and preached every where, the Lord working with them, and confirming the word with signs following. Amen.

Even after Jesus' ascension, He worked with His disciples and confirmed the Word that they preached. The same is true today. When we preach the Word, the power comes to demonstrate and confirm the Word. In Jeremiah, God says, "I watch over My Word and I make it good" (Jer. 1:12, paraphrased). In other words, wherever His Word goes, His power goes to make it good.

GOD SENDS US WITH POWER

God wants to use us, so He sends us out with His power as witnesses of the kingdom. Acts 1:6-8 says,

> *When they therefore were come together, they asked of him, saying, Lord, wilt thou at this time restore again the kingdom to Israel? And he said unto them, It is not for you to know the times or the seasons, which the Father hath put in his own power. But ye shall receive power, after that the Holy Ghost is come upon you: and ye shall be witnesses unto me both in Jerusalem, and in all Judaea, and in Samaria, and unto the uttermost part of the earth.*

Jesus sent out His disciples, but He didn't send them out without the power. When He ascended into heaven, the Holy Spirit came to continue the ministry of Jesus through all believers. Acts 2:1-4 tells of the moment in history when the Holy Spirit would begin this work.

> *And when the day of Pentecost was fully come, they were all with one accord in one place. And suddenly there came*

*a sound from heaven as of a rushing mighty wind, and
it filled all the house where they were sitting. And there
appeared unto them cloven tongues like as of fire, and it
sat upon each of them. And they were all filled with the
Holy Ghost, and began to speak with other tongues, as
the Spirit gave them utterance.*

People from all over the world heard them and were con-
founded because they were speaking in languages that they
never learned, declaring the wonderful works of God. That was
a miracle, a work of God. God knows all of the languages, and
He enabled the people to demonstrate His power by speaking in
new languages. As a result of that, we read in verses 38 and 41,

*Then Peter said unto them, Repent, and be baptized
every one of you in the name of Jesus Christ for the remis-
sion of sins, and ye shall receive the gift of the Holy Ghost.
Then they that gladly received his word were baptized:
and the same day there were added unto them about
three thousand souls.*

After the first miracle that the Holy Spirit worked through
the Church in the book of Acts, three thousand people were
added. Wouldn't it be nice to start a church with three thousand
people? You wouldn't have to send out all those cards and letters
to the zip codes and go on television to tell people, "I'm starting
a church over here. Come out and visit us." We've been trying
to draw people with all this technology, but God has a way that
operates above technology and brings in three thousand members in a moment's time: His mighty power.

In Acts 3, we read about the second miracle of the Holy Spirit through the Church. Peter and John meet a lame man begging at the temple gate, and the man asks them for money. Verses 6-8 tell us what happened.

Then Peter said, Silver and gold have I none; but such as I have give I thee: In the name of Jesus Christ of Nazareth rise up and walk. And he took him by the right hand, and lifted him up: and immediately his feet and ankle bones received strength. And he leaping up stood, and walked, and entered with them into the temple, walking, and leaping, and praising God.

No one could deny this miracle had happened. Here was a man who had never walked and every day had lain at the temple. His relatives probably took him there every day. When Peter and John came to him, he started begging for alms; instead, he got legs that could walk. He had never walked, but now he jumped up, leaped, and praised God. As a result, Acts 4:4 says, "Howbeit many of them which heard the word believed; and the number of the men was about five thousand."

The first time the Holy Spirit performed a miracle and Peter preached, three thousand people were saved. The second time, five thousand were saved. God wants the full gospel. He not only wants to let people know who He is; He also wants them to see what He can do for them. Satan has tried to contain the Church and to keep us from actually operating in the miracles, or the supernatural, of God because he knows that the full gospel is what will bring multitudes into the kingdom.

THE MIRACLE ACTION IS IN THE WORD

Wherever Jesus preached, the anointing of God was there to accomplish what He preached. The power is present to restore, heal, and deliver when we preach the Word of God. God and His power are present when His kingdom is preached.

In the last days, God will work miracles beyond anything we've heard of in our lives, and He'll do them through us. It is a time for miracles. God wants us to develop our faith so He can use us to work miracles in this last hour.

God knows that this world is in trouble. That's why He is sending us into the world. He wants us to walk in His power, show people His goodness supernaturally, and then He can restore the world to Himself. Everything Satan has messed up, God will turn back around. Every person Satan has hurt, God will heal. Every life that has been destroyed, God will restore. It's time for miracles!

In Matthew 24:14, Jesus said, "This gospel of the kingdom shall be preached in all the world for a witness unto all nations; and then shall the end come." When we preach the gospel with demonstration, the devil gets scared because he knows his time is just about over. The more power we demonstrate, the more of a threat we are to him. This is clear in the story of Daniel because the persecution didn't start until the miracles started in his life.

LET THE WORD DO THE WORK

If we have the Word, then we have miracle power. We need to be bold and start speaking from the Spirit and allow the Word to do the work.

My wife was taking some of my shirts to be dry cleaned, and she asked the cashier, "What church do you go to?"

He said, "Well, I don't know."

She said, "You know what? You need to go to church!" She just said what came out of her spirit. When I went back four days later to get my shirts, this cashier saw me and started fidgeting and looking for my shirts. He was so flustered that he dropped the box. Then he looked at me and said, "Your wife told me I need to go to church." Notice, she'd said it four days ago. The anointing, the Holy Spirit, had stayed right on the man morning, noon, and night to confirm the Word that she preached.

The problem has been that the Church has been trying to preach the Word and do the work. We don't need to do the work. God does the work. We just need to believe and act on the Word and expect a miracle.

God is going to use us to bring His supernatural power into this earth. Our days for the natural are over. We're going to think supernaturally. We're going to talk supernaturally. We're going to walk supernaturally. We're going to believe supernaturally. And the world is finally going to see a supernatural Church!

TIME FOR THE MANIFESTATION OF GOD'S CHILDREN

Psalm 82:1 says, "God standeth in the congregation of the mighty; he judgeth among the gods." That word *gods* there is *elohim*. It's not the big God; it's little gods. We are the ones He's talking about. God stands in our midst and judges us. We have the same nature as the big God because we came from the big

God and He made us a little lower than He is (Ps. 8:5). We're in the same class as God. He wants to show people not only who He is but who we are. It is now time for the manifestation of the sons of God.

We have to know who we are.

When the prodigal son asked his father to take him back in as a slave, the father took him back in as a son and gave him the best that he had. The older son said, "Dad, I've done all this right for all these years, and you're giving *him* a party?" He was just like religious people who think they've done everything right.

The father said, "Wait a minute, Son. Don't you see something? All that I have has always been yours." (See Luke 15.) The older brother had been trying to work for it; and like him, we can't work for it. It's by grace that we are saved, healed, delivered, set free—and are witnesses to the world of the kingdom of God in all its power.

Some of us have messed up in life, but we can still go home and God will give us the kingdom. He will use us to demonstrate His power, His love, and His goodness because it's all by His grace as we express our faith in Him. The Father kills the fatted calf (His lamb of God) and cleanses us from all unrighteousness by the blood of Jesus, no matter what we've done. He never stops loving us.

LET THIS MIND BE IN YOU

If we are going to do miracles, we must understand all the authority God has given us and walk confidently in that authority. Jesus

211

told us, "And I will give unto thee the keys of the kingdom of heaven: and whatsoever thou shalt bind on earth shall be bound in heaven: and whatsoever thou shalt loose on earth shall be loosed in heaven" (Matt. 16:19). We need to know that when we bind the devil, he has to remain bound. We speak God's Word and will, the decree goes forth from heaven, the devil is bound, and he cannot cross that line.

The only reason we haven't functioned like this in today's Church is that we haven't known who we are. That's why Paul teaches, "Let this mind be in you, which was also in Christ Jesus" (Phil. 2:5). In other words, he was saying, "The way Jesus thought, we need to think too." Paul writes in Ephesians 5:1 (NKJV), "Therefore be imitators of God as dear children."

We have the mind of Christ (1 Cor. 2:16), but we must choose to function from His mind instead of our natural, carnal, unrenewed thinking. Only with the mind of Christ can we walk in the supernatural power and goodness of God.

WHAT TO DO ABOUT PERSECUTION

As we demonstrate the power of the kingdom, we will face persecution. After Daniel began demonstrating God's power, his critics tried to destroy him by making a law against praying to God Jehovah. I believe in my heart that the devil inspired people to pass the law to take Bibles and prayer out of the United States' public schools because America had demonstrated the power and goodness of God during World War II. The devil used people who had plenty of education but no revelation of God or spiritual truth.

When we follow Jesus, we'll be confronted by the enemy. We can't avoid it. Second Timothy 3:12 says, "Yea, and all that will live godly in Christ Jesus shall suffer persecution." We're going to face some persecution, but when we do it's going to be a time for miracles. It's going to be a time for God to work. We don't need to get scared, and we don't need to back down.

When we get a negative report from the doctor, we cannot just lie down and die. Instead, we need to say, "Okay, Doc, is that your report? Praise God," then call one of the saints and say, "Hey, this man just gave me a bad report. I want you to agree with me that I am healed." It's a time for miracles.

In the book of Daniel, King Darius had signed a law making it illegal to pray to any god or man. Daniel 6:10 says,

> *Now when Daniel knew that the writing was signed, he went into his house; and his windows being open in his chamber toward Jerusalem, he kneeled upon his knees three times a day, and prayed, and gave thanks before his God, as he did aforetime.*

Daniel didn't try to hide his faith. He didn't try to avoid confrontation. He said, "You made the law against my God, so I've got to violate that law." It was a time for miracles, and his faith called God's angel on the scene.

It's a time for miracles in America and in our world. God didn't want the Bible or prayer out of the schools, and He doesn't want the schools teaching our children the world's perverted values. We can't just sit down and let them do that. It's time for the church to rise up and say, "Enough is enough, devil."

We're not blaming or rebuking people; they don't even know what they are doing. We're confronting the enemy and his world system. He can't continue to lie, steal, kill, and destroy because God's kingdom reigns over his kingdom of darkness, and like Daniel, we are going to work God's system.

Daniel's critics threw him in the lions' den, a dark cave, and laid a rock over the opening of it. Yet Daniel didn't fear a bit, because "the people that do know their God shall be strong, and do exploits" (Dan. 11:32). Then the king didn't sleep all night. When people treat us wrong, they can't sleep. They're miserable inside because God says, "Touch not mine anointed, and do my prophets no harm" (Ps. 105:15). The king rose up early in the morning and rolled the stone away. "Daniel? Daniel?" he said.

Daniel replied, "O king, live for ever" (Dan. 6:21).

Daniel worked the system. He knew who his real enemy was and released his faith to defeat him. Jesus said to bless our enemies and pray for those who spitefully use us (Matt. 5:44). That's hard on the flesh, but when we're working miracles, we aren't in the flesh anymore. We're in the spirit. When people persecute us, we bless them. Then God will bless us, and our miracle deliverance will come.

The king asked Daniel, "Did you make it?" (Dan. 6:21.)

Daniel said, "Yes! God sent His angel, and the angel just shut the lions' mouths." He must have read Psalm 34:19 which says, "Many are the afflictions of the righteous, but the Lord shall deliver us out of them all."

Then King Darius wrote a message unto "all people, nations, and languages, that dwell in all the earth."

Peace be multiplied unto you. I make a decree, That in every dominion of my kingdom men tremble and fear before the God of Daniel: for he is the living God, and stedfast for ever, and his kingdom that which shall not be destroyed, and his dominion shall be even unto the end. He delivereth and rescueth, and he worketh signs and wonders in heaven and in earth, who hath delivered Daniel from the power of the lions.

DANIEL 6:25-27

Because Daniel did not back down, because he lived by faith and spoke from the spirit, the whole known earth received the message of the power of God.

It is time for miracles in the earth today. It is time for a manifestation of the sons (mature offspring) of God. Even in the midst of persecution, let us bless people and pray for them and see them be delivered from the kingdom of darkness and translated into the kingdom of His dear Son. Let us seek the kingdom and God's way of doing things, and then watch the world become our inheritance. Let us speak God's Word, manifest the power of His kingdom, and make known God's will on earth as it is in heaven. It is time for the world to see the kingdom of God in us!

ENDNOTES

CHAPTER 2:

1 James Strong, *Exhaustive Concordance of the Bible*, "Greek Dictionary of the New Testament," (Nashville, TN: Thomas Nelson Publishers, 1984), #509.

CHAPTER 3:

1 *The New Bible Commentary: Revised*, Guthrie & Motyer, ed. (Grand Rapids, Michigan: Eerdmans Publishing Co., 1979), p. 691.

2 *Webster's New World College Dictionary*, Third Edition, Victoria Neufeldt, Editor-in-Chief (New York: Macmillan, Inc., 1996), p. 1132.

CHAPTER 4:

1 James Strong, *Exhaustive Concordance of the Bible*, "Hebrew and Chaldee Dictionary," (Nashville, TN: Thomas Nelson Publishers, 1984), #7706.

CHAPTER 9:

1 Meriam-Webster Online Dictionary copyright © 2005 by MerriamWebster, Incorporated, s.v. "dominion."

2 Gwen Shaw, *Redeeming the Land* (Jasper, Arkansas: Engeltal Press, 1987), pp. 37-49, Nimrod and Babylon.

Prayer of Salvation

God loves you—no matter who you are, no matter what your past. God loves you so much that He gave His one and only begotten Son for you. The Bible tells us that "...whoever believes in him shall not perish but have eternal life" (John 3:16 NIV). Jesus laid down His life and rose again so that we could spend eternity with Him in heaven and experience His absolute best on earth. If you would like to receive Jesus into your life, say the following prayer out loud and mean it from your heart.

> *Heavenly Father, I come to You admitting that I am a sinner. Right now, I choose to turn away from sin, and I ask You to cleanse me of all unrighteousness. I believe that Your Son, Jesus, died on the cross to take away my sins. I also believe that He rose again from the dead so that I might be forgiven of my sins and made righteous through faith in Him. I call upon the name of Jesus Christ to be the Savior and Lord of my life. Jesus, I choose to follow You and ask that You fill me with the power of the Holy Spirit. I declare that right now I am*

a child of God. I am free from sin and full of the righteousness of God. I am saved in Jesus' name. Amen.

If you prayed this prayer to receive Jesus Christ as your Savior for the first time, please contact us on the Web at www .billwinston.org to receive a free book.

ABOUT THE AUTHOR

Bill Winston is the founder and senior pastor of Living Word Christian Center in Forest Park, Illinois.

He is also founder of Bill Winston Ministries, a partnership-based outreach ministry; the nationally accredited Joseph Business School; and Faith Ministries Alliance (FMA), an organization of more than 800 churches and ministries. The ministry owns and operates two shopping malls. Bill is married to Veronica and is the father of three and the grandfather of eight.

The Harrison House Vision

Proclaiming the truth and the power

of the Gospel of Jesus Christ with excellence.

Challenging Christians

to live victoriously,

grow spiritually,

know God intimately.

Connect with us on

![f] Facebook @ **HarrisonHousePublishers**

and ![Instagram] Instagram @ **HarrisonHousePublishing**

so you can stay up to date with news

about our books and our authors.

Visit us at **www.harrisonhouse.com**

for a complete product listing as well as

monthly specials for wholesale distribution.